BASIC
for beginners

BASIC

FOR BEGINNERS

Second Edition

Gary G. Bitter

Professor of Education
Arizona State University

Wilson Y. Gateley

QA
76.73
. B3
G 38
1978
C. 2

McGraw-Hill Book Company

New York   St. Louis   San Francisco   Auckland   Bogotá
Düsseldorf   Johannesburg   London   Madrid   Mexico
Montreal   New Delhi   Panama   Paris   São Paulo
Singapore   Sydney   Tokyo   Toronto

Library of Congress Cataloging in Publication Data

Bitter, Gary G.
    Basic for beginners.

    Authors' names appear in reverse order in earlier ed.
    Includes index.
    1. Basic (Computer program language) 2. Time-
sharing computer systems.   I. Gateley, Wilson Y.,
date   joint author. II. Title.
QA76.73.B3G38   1978   001.6'424   77-11054
ISBN 0-07-005492-4

BASIC FOR BEGINNERS

Copyright © 1978, 1970 by McGraw-Hill, Inc. All rights reserved.
Printed in the United States of America. No part of this publication
may be reproduced, stored in a retrieval system, or transmitted, in any
form or by any means, electronic, mechanical, photocopying, record-
ing, or otherwise, without the prior written permission of the publisher.

6 7 8 9 10   BKPBKP   8 6 5 4 3 2

This book was set in Elegante by York Graphic Services, Inc.
The editor was Julienne V. Brown and the production supervisor was
Donna Piligra.
Printed and bound by The Book Press, Inc.

TO

KAY *AND* **KITH**

CONTENTS

PREFACE

This book was written for the purpose of providing a self-instructional manual for students. The need for such a manual arose because teachers in many courses in which profitable use of a computer might be made could not afford the time to teach programming within the course and were reluctant to require a formal programming course as a prerequisite. The manual was designed to provide a student with the capability for writing simple programs and going through the mechanics needed to process them on a time-sharing computing system. The book has been used successfully by thousands of students including elementary; high school; high school teachers; college students taking courses in mathematics, physics, chemistry, genetics, and political science; and college teachers. The manual requires about ten hours of the student's time and about one hour of computer terminal time to complete.

Because of the many versions of the BASIC language and the several types of terminals which might be used, the book avoids, for the most part, the special characteristics of a given system. We strongly recommend that the person in charge of the terminals prepare a one- or two-page handout explaining the exact details of calling the computer and listing the most frequently used system commands. In addition, the appropriate manuals for both the terminal and the language should be made readily available for use by the students.

We have found that student assistants can be of great help in easing the fears of beginners when they first confront a terminal and in answering some of the simple questions which inevitably arise.

For a fair assessment of the book, it is necessary to keep in mind what it is designed to do and what it is not designed to do. The prime purpose is to provide a simple, easily understood introduction to the BASIC language so that students can make use of a terminal facility as a tool within the framework of other courses with varying subject matter. In addition, the book is designed to be "done" from beginning to end in a relatively short period of time and with no, or at least minimal, supervision. It is not intended to be exhaustive or even particularly comprehensive, and students finishing it will still have much to learn if they desire to become experts in the language.

One consequence of our objectives is the relatively small number of exercises within the main text. We are well aware that in general they are not sufficient to develop any high degree of proficiency on the part of students. Nevertheless we have found that this limited number is adequate in preparing students to move on to subject matter-oriented problems with little difficulty. For those who need or wish additional practice, a collection of extra problems to be programmed is included in Appendix B.

We have deviated in two places in including those aspects of the language common to all versions. First, we have put in a short section dealing with string data; and second, we have not covered the GØSUB and RETURN statements. In the former case we have observed that a computer's ability to deal with nonnumeric symbols is frequently unknown to beginning students and also that students get a great deal of pleasure and motivation in writing programs which involve manipulations of such data. The deletion of the GØSUB and RETURN statements is certainly questionable but was made because of our feeling that the subroutine concept, although admittedly of great usefulness in complicated programs, is of little value in most beginner's programs and is more likely to confuse than to help the novice.

P.S. Since this book is self-instructional, home computer enthusiasts will find it invaluable as a source to learn BASIC.

Gary G. Bitter
Wilson Y. Gateley

ACKNOWLEDGMENTS

The authors express their thanks to the Colorado College students and faculty and to the computer manufacturers who have contributed so much in making this text possible. The authors' gratitude is also expressed to their patient wives as well as to Doris A. Ogden and Rita Jackson, who typed the manuscript.

Gary G. Bitter
Wilson Y. Gateley

1

the beginning

1.1 What and Why

This book is a self-instructional manual which will get you started in learning the art and science of computer programming. By working through it thoroughly and carefully you should attain a working knowledge of the programming language BASIC. At that point you should be in a position to make substantial use of a time-sharing computer system to help you solve a wide variety of problems in many subjects. You should be forewarned, however, that what you learn from this book is just a start; knowing English does not imply that a person can write a good story, and knowing BASIC does not imply that a person can write a good computer program. But one must start somewhere, and that's what this book is all about.

There are many reasons why one would want to learn to write computer programs. Computers are playing an important role in our world today, and that importance will inevitably increase. Consequently it seems desirable that every person know something, preferably from actual experience, about these machines. On a more contemplative plane, computers open up for consideration a tremendous range of new problems in almost every subject and give the student a chance to explore questions which only a short time ago were unexplorable by anyone. A computer can also help in the solution of many familiar problems, and considerable time and money can frequently be saved by judicious use of a machine. Finally, computer programming is, for most people, a lot of fun.

1.2 Programs and Algorithms

A computer program is an explicit set of instructions for performing certain tasks or for solving a certain problem and is written and communicated in a language and form comprehensible to the computer. There is nothing very mysterious in this definition; and if you replace the word "computer" by "person," it is nothing more than a definition of, say, a recipe, a law, or the piece of paper that tells you how to assemble a model airplane. Nevertheless a few comments are in order.

First, the word "explicit" is vital. It rightly suggests a computer has neither imagination nor intuition. Consequently each and every step of the program must be spelled out in frequently exasperating detail. A common sin of most beginners is to omit from a program certain instructions which would be obvious and hence unstated if one were dealing with an intelligent human being but which must be carefully included when a computer is involved. Second, the language and grammar one uses with a computer are strictly determined by the computer itself, and no give-and-take can be expected by the programmer. If the computer demands, say, a comma in a certain place in a certain instruction, the comma must be there even though to any reasonable person the meaning is clear without the comma. This necessity for absolute adherence to more or less arbitrary rules is sometimes frustrating but is simply one of the facts of life one must submit to in order to make successful use of a computer.

It should be emphasized that even though any computer is able to understand several different "languages," it does so only one at a time; using parts of different computer languages in one program is forbidden. If you are ignorant of any computer language at this point, this cautionary note may of course be ignored; but if you are acquainted with FORTRAN, for example, be careful not to mix its vocabulary and grammar with the similar but not identical aspects of BASIC.

Finally, and associated with the necessity for detail, there is the desirability for logical completeness of a program. We mean by this the provision for handling as many logical contingencies in the problem as possible. Sometimes completeness is not necessary, but one should always be aware of situations for which explicit provisions have not been made. For example, a program to compute the roots of a quadratic equation is easier to write if one ignores the possibility of imaginary roots and is perfectly satisfactory as long as such an equation doesn't occur; if one does, however, the computer will be at a loss as to what to do and will either reject the program or produce some completely erroneous and irrelevant results (commonly known as "garbage"). The majority of spectacular computer "accidents" which are exploited in the newspapers—where someone received sixteen bills for a single purchase or a person's bank account was unexpectedly increased by a million dollars—are due to the failure, not of a computer, but of a programmer who didn't allow for some unlikely situation which finally occurred. Such lapses in writing programs will probably cause only minor inconveniences for you, but don't be too surprised when they show up.

It is sometimes convenient to distinguish between the method of solving a problem and a program for actually doing so. The method itself is called an "algorithm" and differs from a program in that it is essentially "language-free" and is not concerned with minor programming details such as how the data will be put into the computer or how the final answers will be printed out. By language-free we mean that for the purpose of describing the algorithm the set of instructions can be written or presented in any convenient manner. An algorithm may be given by a series of one or more mathematical formulas, by a diagram, by a verbal description, or, most commonly, by a combination of these methods. ("Flow diagrams," which will be discussed in a later chapter, are frequently used for displaying an algorithm.) It is sometimes desirable to break the writing of computer programs into two phases: first, analysis of the problem and obtaining an appropriate algorithm; and, second, putting the algorithm into a language comprehensible to a computer and supplying the programming details. Although in many cases the two phases are performed almost simultaneously and by the same person, they frequently can be kept separate and carried out by different individuals. One important advantage of such a separation is that once the algorithm is finished, a program can be written for any computer by a person who may have relatively little knowledge of how and why the algorithm works.

1.3 The Computer

Although the details of the construction and operation of an overall computer system are no direct concern of this book, a few comments may help you become oriented to the machine with which you will be conversing and to the procedures used to run programs. But remember a computer is a machine that processes information much the same as an oil refinery processes oil.

Figure 1.1 gives a rough idea of the functional construction of a computer. The arrows show the direction of the flow of the sequences of electrical pulses which repre-

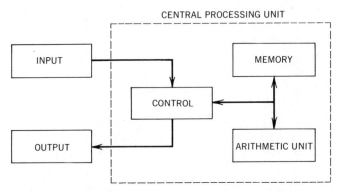

FIGURE 1.1   **Functional Diagram of a Simple Computer System**

sent the information being sent from one point to another. A specific set of instructions called a program and any associated data are introduced into the computer by an input unit which converts the given information—for example, alphabetic or numeric symbols—into the appropriate sequences of electrical pulses. This information passes into the control unit which directs all the computer's activities. On the basis of at least part of the input information, the control unit decides what must be done and by using the memory unit (for storing the program and data until needed) and the arithmetic unit (which performs the actual arithmetic and logical operations as called for by the program) causes the program to be executed. When the execution of the program generates some output data (answers), the data are sent to the output unit where the representation of the information is changed to a form intelligible to a human.

Generally the computer would solve $2 + 3 =$ as shown at the top of the next page. This seems complicated, but remember that the computer does this routinely in

Input

Store

Compute

Store

Output

thousandths of a second. The main idea is that the computer follows only the directions provided or directions built into the computer system.

Commonly used input/output devices include punch card readers, optical scanners (for reading handwritten or printed characters), high-speed printers, automatic plotters, cathode ray tubes (CRT), visual display units, electric type-writers, and Teletypes.

The control, memory, and arithmetic units can be thought of as constituting a single unit which we will refer to as the central processing unit (CPU).

At this point we are in a position to indicate the difference between "hardware" and "software," two terms you are certain to encounter if you have much contact with computers. Every computer contains a collection of electronic components which function in such a manner as to add two numbers; this unit, the accumulator or adder, is part of the computer's hardware because it is made up of physical devices. Now, how about multiplication? This can be handled in two ways: first, a physical device can be constructed to perform the operation; or, second, we can make use of the fact that multiplication can be performed by repeated additions and write a small program which will perform multiplication by using the adder. This program can be stored in the computer's memory and called upon as needed. In the former case multiplication is done by hardware and in the latter, by software. In general the term "software" is used to indicate a computer program which remains within the computer and is used either automatically or upon request by a programmer. As computers have grown in size and complexity, the production of suitable software has become a major task; and although putting a price on any program is difficult to do, the cost of software in a modern computer system may equal or even exceed the cost of the hardware.

The computer system described above executes one program at a time and is rather inefficient because the speed of the CPU in executing programs is far greater than the speeds of most input/output units. For example, a computer could perform a million or so additions during the time required to write your name with a typewriter. Consequently the CPU may remain idle for a large fraction of the total time between input and output. To increase the

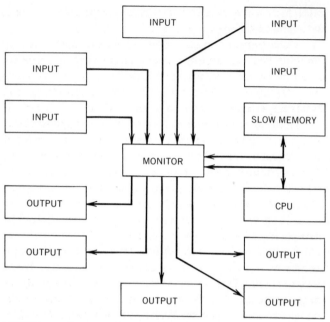

FIGURE 1.2   **Computer System with a Monitor**

efficiency of the system, a device called a "monitor" or "executive" is used. The monitor is essentially a mechanized computer operator capable of directing the operations of several input and output units as well as the CPU and of doing this at speeds which are comparable with that of the CPU itself. The word "mechanized" is used here in a very general sense because the monitor is constructed mostly of software rather than hardware.

A diagram of a computer system with a monitor is shown in Figure 1.2. As indicated in the figure, the monitor usually operates in conjunction with a "slow" memory unit (one or more magnetic disks, drums, or tape units). This memory is distinct from the "fast" memory located in the CPU and normally has a much greater capacity. It is slow in the sense that more time is needed both to locate the place within the memory in which certain information is to be stored or extracted and to move information into or out of the memory. Even a slow memory is extremely fast, however, compared to that of a man; the "access" time for a human memory is measured in seconds, for a slow computer memory in thousandths of a second, and for a fast computer memory in millionths of a second.

The function of the slow memory is to store, temporarily, programs and data which come from the input units and results which are to go to the output units. This storage, controlled by the monitor, permits the slow memory to act like extremely fast input/output units as far as the CPU is concerned, and very little CPU time is lost in exchanging information between the CPU and the slow memory.

With a monitored system, several input and output devices can operate simultaneously (five of each are shown in Figure 1.2, but there may be many more). Therefore, as long as there are enough programs to be processed, the CPU can be kept busy, resulting in an efficient and economical operation.

The terms "batch-processing" and "time-sharing" refer to the manner in which a monitored computer executes a program. In the batch-processing mode each program is executed from beginning to end without pause, whereas in the time-sharing mode several programs are in various stages of execution at the same time. Time-sharing is accomplished by doing a little work on one program, then a little on another one, and so forth. After each of a group of programs has had one turn, the computer goes back to the first one and repeats the cycle. This cycling continues indefinitely; when one program is finished, it is replaced by another one. The keys to the success of this procedure are the monitor, which controls the length of time the CPU works on each program, and the slow memory, which holds each partially executed program until its next turn arrives.

It is important to note that the swapping of programs

between the slow memory and the CPU does take some time (called "overhead"). As a result, time-sharing is less efficient than batch-processing in making full use of the CPU when executing long programs. One big advantage of time-sharing comes from the fact that many programs can be put into the computer from very slow input devices such as Teletypes or cathode ray tubes operated by humans. Because of the tremendous speed of the computer and its ability to work on each of many programs a little at a time, it appears to a user that the computer is devoting all of its time to his/her particular program. A second advantage is that a user is able to interact with the computer while his/her program is being processed; thus, if he/she has made mistakes or wishes to alter a program, he/she may do so while the program is still in the computer. This feature usually leads to a great reduction in the total time required to write, correct ("debug"), and execute a program. In batch-processing, the computer program is usually input into the computer via data cards. But, in time-sharing, the information is usually input into the computer by typing the program on a Teletype or CRT. Compared to batch-processing, time-sharing is much more conservative of the user's time and is well suited to the philosophy that a computer should be the servant of man rather than the reverse.

It must be realized, however, that programs which require a large amount of CPU time are generally ill suited to a time-sharing system. For example, a program which requires one hour of CPU time might in a time-sharing system be swapped between the slow memory and the CPU several thousand times (hence high overhead costs) and might require several hours to execute because of sharing the CPU with other programs. The programs to be written for this course of study should seldom require more than a few seconds of CPU time to execute, and this will be true for a large percentage of the programs you will write in the future. The actual time to process a program will of course be longer because you will be sharing, or more accurately, splitting time with several other users. If you do encounter a problem which requires many minutes or even hours of CPU time to solve, you might consider finding a batch-processing system, although the initial writing and debugging could still be done using time-sharing.

With current time-sharing computer systems the most common input/output device is either a Teletype or similar typewriterlike device or a Cathode Ray Tube (CRT). A CRT is like a TV and provides only a video display. Therefore the programmer has no printed copy of his/her work. The number of terminals which can be connected to the computer simultaneously depends upon the particular computer, but 20 to 100 is a common number, and up to several thousand may be possible in the near future. The terminals may be wired directly to the computer, but more commonly they communicate by telephone lines which go to an automatic switchboard, which in turn is connected to the computer. With this arrangement, any number of terminals may have access to the computer, and a terminal may be located several thousand miles away from the computer itself.

One major disadvantage of the present-day terminals is their relatively slow information transfer rate. A typical terminal is capable of input or output at about 600 characters (letters, numerals, or special symbols) per minute. While this is considerably faster than most people can type, it is very slow compared to a high-speed printer or card reader which may operate at 100,000 characters per minute. This is of no consequence for the programs you will be writing for this course of study but may become a major problem afterward. If it does, see your computer director for suggestions.

1.4   Computer Languages

As indicated above, the fundamental language or method of representing information in a computer is a collection of electrical pulses. A computer recognizes both the presence and the absence of a pulse, and this gives rise to the so-called binary representation. For example, if 0 represents the absence of a pulse and 1 its presence, a sequence such as 01101001 will generally have some specific meaning for a computer.

It is possible to write programs and represent any data from your age to one of Shakespeare's plays in binary notation. In fact in the early days of computers, twenty years or so ago, it was necessary to do so. At the best, however, binary notation is extremely inconvenient and laborious to use. If this were still the only way to communicate with computers, there would undoubtedly be a much smaller number of them in use today.

The computer language problem has been solved by some very ingenious pieces of software, called "compilers," which in effect translate from certain man-made languages to the inherent binary language of the computer. The compiler has brought the art of programming within reach of everyone.

There are still problems however. A computer is a superrational device, and the ambiguities and impreciseness of human languages such as English and French make these languages very unsuitable for use with a computer. Consequently new languages have been constructed which are easily used by humans and are coherent and free of contradictions and ambiguities, both in vocabulary and grammar. Unfortunately inventing a new language and building the necessary compiler to go with it are not easy tasks. Therefore all such languages are much more restricted than human ones and are generally designed for special purposes. Because there are so many special purposes to be served and any two language inventors will usually have different ideas about how to serve even one purpose, a veritable babel of computer programming languages has evolved over the past ten or fifteen years, and there is no end in sight. Among the better known languages are BASIC, FORTRAN, COBOL, PL-1, ALGOL, SNOBOL, APL, LISP, and MAD. Of these, BASIC is one of the most common. We might mention the completely unimportant fact that each of these names is an acronym. Thus BASIC is "Beginner's All-purpose Symbolic Instruction Code," FORTRAN is "FORmula TRANslation," ALGOL is "ALGOrithmic Language," etc.

The language BASIC was originally developed several years ago at Dartmouth College specifically for time-sharing purposes and is now the most widely used language for time-sharing. (FORTRAN, developed in the 1950s, is similar to BASIC in many respects and is the most popular language for use with batch-processing systems.) The spread of BASIC from the original Dartmouth–General Electric system to other computer systems has produced a fairly large number of "dialects" of the language. This diversity and the changes that are constantly taking place to improve the power and convenience of the language, make it impossible to write a book which is both comprehensive and accurate. Consequently, we have selected for the most part, only those aspects of BASIC which are common to all dialects.

1.5   Using the Book

Because this book has been written to serve as a do-it-yourself manual, a few comments about its use are in order.

Most of the chapters contain explanatory material, a set of questions, and at least one exercise for which you are to write a program to be processed on the computer. To get the most out of this book it is necessary to read everything, answer all the questions, and do several of the exercises.

You will find the answers to questions at the end of each question section. Make an honest effort to give an answer to each question before looking at the one in the book; if yours is different, find out why.

We have included relatively few exercises within the main body of the text in order that there can be no question as to which ones to do; that is, do all of them. If you have the time, inclination, and access to a computer after you finish the book, you might be interested in trying some of the additional exercises in Appendix B. These illustrate different applications and will occasionally strain your ingenuity.

It will usually pay to *reread* most of the material at least once. Small and apparently unimportant details can easily escape your attention the first time, but it is frequently these details that make the difference between a program which works and one which doesn't.

There are several points in the text which differ among various BASIC dialects. Please refer to the manufacturer's BASIC manual for specific answers on dialect. If you cannot find the manufacturer's manual ask your computer director to furnish the necessary information.

Finally, don't hesitate to seek help. Sources of aid include fellow students, teachers, your computer director, and the terminal and BASIC manuals produced by the manufacturer of your system (copies of these manuals should be available close to your terminal). One more source is the book *BASIC Programming* by John G. Kemeny and Thomas E. Kurtz (Wiley, 1975). These authors are the original BASIC experts, as they directed the development of the language at Dartmouth College. Reference to their book is particularly recommended because they have included a large number of complete programs which involve problems from a wide range of applications.

2

getting started

2.1 Introduction

Getting started involves the ability to sign on to the computer and using the terminal. This chapter will familiarize you with common remote terminals used in a time-sharing computer system. An actual sign on procedure, illustrating the mechanics and vocabulary needed to communicate with a time-sharing computer, is explained step by step. But this sample is for illustrative purposes and more than likely your sign on procedure will be different. After completing this chapter check with your instructor or computer center personnel for sign on procedures and do exercise one.

2.2 The Terminal*

Figures 2.1 to 2.3 show three popular terminals. They are all similar in function, and each contains a typewriterlike keyboard and a mechanism for producing a written copy of what is typed by the user or what is sent to the user by the computer. A terminal differs from an ordinary typewriter in that striking a key on the keyboard produces a coded electrical signal which may be sent to the computer. The

*See Appendix A for details of using the ASR 33 Teletype (Figure 2.1).

FIGURE 2.1   **Courtesy of Teletype Corp.**

printing mechanism of the terminal may also be operated
by electrical signals sent from the computer. In addition to
the printing mechanism, a terminal has several control
keys, buttons, or switches, and some have a device to
punch and read paper tape.

FIGURE 2.2   **Portable Terminal Courtesy of Texas Instruments.**

Figures 2.4 to 2.7 show four Cathode Ray Tube (CRT) terminals. They are similar in function and each has a television (video) display. This terminal differs from the typewriter type in Figures 2.1 to 2.3 in that it gives no written ("hard copy") of what is typed in or received from the computer.

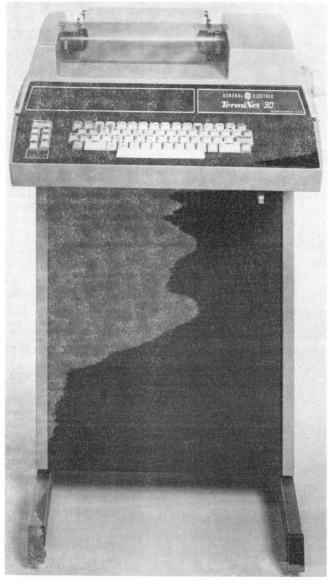

FIGURE 2.3   Courtesy of General Electric Corp.

FIGURE 2.4 Courtesy of Infoton Corp.

FIGURE 2.5 Courtesy of Digital Equipment Corp.

FIGURE 2.6   **Courtesy of IBM**

Figure 2.8 is a typical terminal keyboard.

The terminal symbols used in this book are as follows (locate them on the keyboard):

    the 10 numerals, 0 through 9
    the 26 letters, A through Z
    the punctuation symbols:

FIGURE 2.7   **Courtesy of Hazeltine Corp.**

.   period
,   comma
;   semicolon
"   (double) quotation marks
(left parenthesis
)   right parenthesis

the special symbols:

↑   upward arrow
←   left arrow
$ dollar sign
+   plus
−   minus
*   asterisk
/   slash
<   less than
>   greater than
=   equals
    space

Keyboard

FIGURE 2.8   **Typical Terminal Keyboard**

2.3   A Short Program

In this section we will describe the mechanics of processing a simple BASIC program. Figure 2.9 shows the printout of the entire operation of one type of computer. Remember to check with your computer director for the details to sign on your computer system. This printout has been edited by adding circled numbers in front of certain lines or groups of lines for reference in the discussion below and by underlining that portion of the printout which is generated by the computer. Hence the computer typed the underlined part and the user typed the rest.

This program was processed using a time-sharing computer. The terminal was located at Hoisington, Kansas, and the computer was at Arizona State University in Tempe, Arizona. The terminal and computer were connected by regular telephone lines.

The BASIC program for the example consists of the following four statements:

```
10 LET X=25
20 LET Y=15
30 PRINT X,Y,X+Y,X−Y,X*Y
40 END
```

① ASU35478

② TIME—SHARING SERVICE

 ØN AT 17:56 PX SYSF 2/2/78 TTY 17

③ ACCØUNT NUMBER—EDBITTER
④ PRØJECT ID—2ED691
⑤ SYSTEM—BASIC
⑥ NEW ØR ØLD—NEW
⑦ NEW FILE NAME—GARY
⑧ READY.

 10 LET X=25
⑨ 20 LET Y=15
 30 PRINT X,Y,X+Y,X-Y,X*Y
 40 END
⑩ RUN

⑪ GARY 17:58 PX SYSF 2/2/78

⑫ 25   15   40   10   375

⑬ USED 2.00 UNITS.
⑭ LIST

⑮ GARY 17:58 PX SYSF 2/2/78

⑯ 10 LET X=25
⑯ 20 LET Y=15
 30 PRINT X,Y,X+Y,X-Y,X*Y
 40 END

⑰ BYE

⑱ *** ØFF AT 17:58 ELAPSED TERMINAL TIME = 1 MIN.

FIGURE 2.9 **Printout of a Program Run**

  The exact meaning and form of each statement will
be discussed in detail in the next chapter. It should be fairly
apparent what is being done, however: the variables X and
Y are first assigned the values of 25 and 15 respectively,

and these values, together with the values of $X+Y$, $X-Y$, and $X*Y$, are printed, that is, typed by the computer. Obviously it is not a very profound program, but we are using it just to give the computer something to do while we demonstrate the mechanics of the conversation. One important point about the program can be made here: the BASIC statements which are preceded by the numbers 10, 20, 30, and 40 must begin with such a number. Line numbers will be discussed more thoroughly in the next chapter. We mention them here to point out the distinction between program statements (which have line numbers) and system commands (which do not). In general, system commands form the dialogue between the user and the monitor in the computer and are concerned with housekeeping details and discussion *about* the program, whereas the program statements, written in BASIC, are translated into machine language and executed within the CPU. System commands will be discussed at greater length in the next section after we have seen a few of them at work.

Now let's consider the details of the whole operation which produced Figure 2.9. The first action was by the user and consisted of dialing the call number of the computer. Now look at Figure 2.9.

1 The computer apparently typed this code name; actually it was produced by the terminal itself in response to a query from the computer to determine which terminal was calling. The code name, called the "answer back" code, identifies the particular terminal, and the computer will refuse to deal with a terminal whose answer back code has not been previously authorized.

2 The computer then sent some miscellaneous information including its name (TIME-SHARING SERVICE), the time of day (17:56), the date (2/2/78), and some completely irrelevant details.

3 The computer asked for the account number, which identifies the user in the same manner as the answer back code identifies the terminal. The user responded with his/her number (EDBITTER). An unauthorized number will cause the computer to terminate the conversation. After the user typed his/her number, he/she struck the RETURN key on the terminal. This moved the print head back to the left side of the paper and also told the computer that the user had finished typing the required information. The computer acknowledged the receipt of the RETURN signal by sending a LINE FEED signal which advanced the paper in the terminal one line. Please note carefully that the use of the RETURN is mandatory at the conclusion of every message (system command or program statement) typed by the user.

4 The computer asked for a project identification code. This code is used for billing purposes and is not used on many systems.

5 The computer asked for the language (SYSTEM) which the user wanted to use. The user responded with BASIC.

6 The computer asked if the program was a NEW or ØLD one. An ØLD program is one which was put into the computer at an earlier time and saved in a file in the computer's memory. In our example the user was starting from scratch and so responded NEW.

7 The computer asked for the FILE NAME, which is the name the user wishes to give to the program. More accurately, the FILE NAME is the name of a portion of the computer's slow memory where the program is to be stored, but from

the user's viewpoint the distinction is irrelevant. The names which are permissible differ from system to system, but in almost all systems a name consisting of up to six letters is allowed. In our example the user called the program GARY.

8 The computer said READY, which indicated it was ready to continue and was waiting for the user's next instruction.

9 The user now typed in the program. Remember that after each line is typed, the RETURN key must be depressed.

10 After typing the program, the user typed RUN, which told the computer to start executing the program. Do not confuse the system command RUN with our use of the same word in referring to the overall process of calling up the computer and putting in and executing a program.

11 The computer responded with a heading which included the name of the program and some other information.

12 The computer printed the output of the program, in this case the data and computations requested in line 30 of the program.

13 This line indicated the program execution was completed and that 2.00 units were used. A unit is a measurement of time and facilities (units vary with computer manufacturers) used by the computer in executing the program. The number of units is used in making up the bill for computer-use charges at most installations.

14 The user gave the command LIST, which asks the computer to print a copy of the program. The value of this command will become apparent in section 2.5, which includes a discussion of

the correction of errors. If a program has not been changed since it was first typed into the computer, there is no point in asking for a listing unless the user suspects a communication error was made—that is, the program was garbled when it was sent to the computer. This is not a common occurrence but does happen occasionally. In our example the listing corresponds exactly to what was originally typed in.

15 First the computer typed a heading which included the name of the program and some other details of no importance.

16 The computer then typed a copy of the program.

17 The user had finished and typed BYE.

18 The computer then terminated the communication and typed the time of day and the total amount of terminal time used since the conversation began (this time is normally used in billing).

2.4 System Commands

In addition to the system commands which were used in the example in the last section, there are several others which you will need. We will not attempt to make a comprehensive listing of all possible commands because of the variation between systems and the lack of need in this book for some of the more sophisticated ones. After you become acquainted with your system, you may wish to look into your terminal manual and discover just what is available.

It is convenient to separate system commands into two classes, computer commands and user commands, the adjective indicating the source of the command. Thus in our example the computer commands included ACCOUNT NUMBER, PRØJECT ID, SYSTEM, NEW ØR

ØLD, NEW FILE NAME, and READY. The user commands
were RUN, LIST, and BYE.

Figures 2.10 and 2.11 illustrate the use of the two very
valuable user commands SAVE and UNSAVE. The conversation in Figure 2.10 starts out exactly as that in Figure
2.11, but after the program has been typed in, the user
command SAVE is sent to the computer. On receipt of this
command the computer copies the program from the
"working" file (where it is being worked on) into a "permanent" file in the computer's slow memory. This copy of
the program will then remain in the permanent file for use
at any time in the future or until we tell the computer to
erase (UNSAVE) it. This ability to store a program indefinitely within the computer is useful in two situations: first,
when the program has some errors in it and we need some
time to think before trying to correct it; and, second, when

FIGURE 2.10   **Saving a Program**

ASU35478

TIME-SHARING SERVICE

ØN AT 7:59   PX SYSF 2/2/78   TTY 17

ACCOUNT NUMBER—EDBITTER
PRØJECT ID—2ED691
SYSTEM—BASIC
NEW ØR ØLD—NEW
NEW FILE NAME—GARY
READY.

10 LET X=25
20 LET Y=15
30 PRINT X,Y,X+Y,X-Y,X*Y
40 END
SAVE
WAIT.

READY.

BYE

***   ØFF AT 8:01   ELAPSED TERMINAL TIME =   1 Min.

we wish to use the same program repeatedly day after day. In either case storing the program eliminates the necessity of typing it in each time we need it.

The computer command WAIT occurs in Figure 2.10. Its meaning is the obvious one, and it may appear in many

```
ASU35478


TIME-SHARING SERVICE


ØN AT  8:01  PX SYSF 2/2/78  TTY 17

ACCØUNT NUMBER—EDBITTER
PRØJECT ID—2ED691
SYSTEM—BASIC
NEW ØR ØLD—ØLD
ØLD FILE NAME—GARY
WAIT.

READY.

RUN


GARY    8:02   PX SYSF 2/2/78

25       15       40       10        375


USED    2.33 UNITS.
LISTNH

10 LET X=25
20 LET Y=15
30 PRINT X,Y,X+Y,X-Y,X*Y
40 END


UNSAVE
READY.

BYE

***ØFF AT  8:03  ELAPSED TERMINAL TIME =    1 Min.
```

FIGURE 2.11 **Using a Saved Program**

places. Its occurrence generally depends upon how many
people are using the computer—the more people, the more
WAITs. The READY following the SAVE and WAIT tells
the user that the SAVE command has been carried out.

Figure 2.11 shows how a saved program is called.
During the initial dialogue the reply of ØLD is made to
the computer command NEW ØR ØLD. The computer then
asks ØLD FILE NAME, and the user responds with the
proper name—that is, the name which was used during the
run in which the program was saved. The computer then
responds (possibly after a WAIT) with READY, which
indicates the program has been copied from the permanent
file into the working file and is ready to be executed or
modified. In this example the program was first executed
(observe that the program output is identical to that in
Figure 2.9 and then listed. The list command LISTNH is
slightly different from the one used earlier (LIST). The NH
on the end means "no heading" and you see that the heading is not present in Figure 2.11. The usefulness of this
modification, other than saving a few seconds of time, will
be seen in Appendix A.

Finally in Figure 2.11 the user command UNSAVE
is given. This tells the computer to erase the copy of the
program from the permanent file, and the computer responds with READY when this has been done. It should
be noted that even after the UNSAVE has been acted upon,
a copy of the program still exists in the working file of the
computer and may be executed or modified as usual.

The majority of the remaining computer commands
are clear in meaning and should give you no trouble. If an
improper response is made to a computer command—for
example, a misspelled word—the computer will type
WHAT? Usually, if the response is retyped correctly, processing will proceed normally.

Several programs may be worked upon one after
another during the same run by means of the user command NEW or ØLD. When the computer receives one of

these, the working file is cleared, and the computer command NEW FILE NAME or ØLD FILE NAME is sent back. The user may then proceed in the usual way.

2.5 Correcting Errors

One of the evils of being human is that one makes mistakes. Time-sharing computer systems recognize this characteristic of a user and make available three methods of correcting errors: using the left arrow (the upper symbol on the O key), using the ESC key (ALT MODE, DELETE or RUB-OUT on some terminals) and retyping a program line.

The left arrow acts like a backspace key which also erases the character spaced over. This backspacing takes place within the computer and not physically on the printout on the Teletype. Thus the typed message AB←C produces the actual message AC. The arrow may be used repeatedly if desired; thus typing ABC←←DE produces ADE. This method of correction is very useful since many typing errors are detected the instant they are made, and it may be used while preparing paper tapes as well as online.

The ESC key is used only during online operation and is of value when a user command needs to be corrected or changed before the terminating RETURN is sent. If the ESC key is pushed, the computer will type DELETED on the same line and then go to the beginning of the next line.

A program statement, which has a line number, may be replaced within the computer by typing another statement with the same line number. When this is done, the computer replaces the first statement with the second. This method may be used either to correct typing or logical errors or to change one or several statements of a working program. A program statement may be deleted entirely by typing its line number followed by a RETURN.

If you make several changes or corrections to a

program, it may be desirable to list the program in order
to see what the current version actually is. When giving
a listing, the computer will produce a cleaned-up copy.

Figure 2.12 is the printout of our example program
in a run which included several errors. The computer's
typing is underlined. The following points should be noted:

1 An invalid account number was typed by the
   user. The computer said so, the user typed the
   correct number, and the run proceeded.

2 The user reply to SYSTEM was BAS rather than
   BASIC, and the abbreviation was accepted by the
   computer. Many user commands can be given by
   using only the first three letters. This is of course
   a minor detail but one which can speed up the
   routine mechanics a little bit.

3 When typing the first line of the program, the user
   forgot temporarily to put in a line number (a fairly
   common error). The error was caught after typing
   the letters LE, so the left arrow was used twice
   to erase the two letters. If more of the line had
   been typed before detecting the error, it would
   have been easier to delete the line by the ESC key.
   If the line had been neither corrected nor deleted,
   the computer would have interpreted it as a user
   command because it did not start with a number;
   the "command" would have been meaningless
   (probably) to the computer, and it would have
   responded with WHAT?.

4 The word PRINT in line 30 of the program was
   misspelled PREMT, and the error was not caught
   during the typing of the program. After the RUN
   command was given, the computer printed a diagnostic message which indicated the location of
   the error. The offending line was then typed cor-

ASU35478

TIME-SHARING SERVICE

ØN AT   8:02   PX SYSF 2/17/78   TTY 17

① ACCØUNT NUMBER--EDBITTR
   INCØRRECT FØRMAT- RETYPE IT--EDBITTER
   PRØJECT ID--2ED691
② SYSTEM--BAS
   NEW ØR ØLD--NEW
   NEW FILE NAME--MISTAKE
   READY.

③ LE←←10 LET X=25
   20 LET Y=15
④ 30 PREMT X,Y,X+Y,X−Y,X*Y
   40 END
⑤ RIN
   WHAT?
   RUN

⑥ MISTAK   8:04   PX SYSF 2/17/78

   ILLEGAL INSTRUCTIØN   IN   30

   USED   0.83 UNITS.
   30 PRINT X,Y,X+Y,X−Y,X*Y
   RUN

   MISTAK   8:05 PX SYSF 2/17/78

   25   15   40   10   375

   USED   1.50 UNITS.
⑦ LASTNH DELETED
   LISTNH

   10 LET X=25
   20 LET Y=15
   30 PRINT X,Y,X+Y,X−Y,X*Y
   40 END

   BYE

   *** ØFF AT 8:05   ELAPSED TERMINAL TIME=   2 MIN.

FIGURE 2.12

rectly, and the program was executed satisfactorily.

5 The user command RUN was misspelled RIN.
This was unintelligible to the computer, and it
responded WHAT?. The user then typed RUN,
and the computer carried on.

6 The program name was originally given as MIS-
TAKE. Note on the run heading that the computer
took only the first six letters of the word as the
official name of the program.

7 After the successful run of the program, the user
wished to get a listing of the program. He first
typed LASTNH, noticed his mistake, pushed the
ESC key (to which the computer responded DE-
LETED), and finally typed LISTNH. Observe that
the listed version of the program, which is the one
in the working file of the computer, has been
cleaned up by the correction of the initial errors
in lines 10 and 30.

For more system commands, see Appendix D.

2.6 Exercise

The purpose of this exercise is to get you familiar
with both your terminal and your computer. If your system
differs very much from the one used in this chapter, you
may need some help to get the details straightened out.
Above all, don't be afraid of hurting or being hurt by either
the terminal or the computer. The computer is well beyond
your reach; and, unless you use a hammer instead of your
fingers, there is little chance of your damaging the terminal.

1 Run from start to finish the sample program used
in this chapter.

a start at
BASIC

3.1 Introduction

In this chapter we finally get down to learning something
about BASIC. All of the statements used in our example
program in Chapter 2 will be explained in detail, and the
fundamental concepts of "constants" and "variables" will
be explained. Please do not gloss over the explanations of
these concepts, because they are of the utmost importance,
and a clear understanding of them will prevent many
difficulties later on.

3.2 Constants

A computer program may be viewed as a set of instructions
for manipulating a collection of numbers, letters, or other
symbols. This collection is called "data." In many problems
the data consist entirely of numbers, and so numeric data
are our first concern. Some versions of BASIC also permit
manipulation of nonnumeric data, but we will postpone
discussion of this until Chapter 7. We shall refer to a specific number, such as 13, −17.2, or 3.14159, as a "con-

stant." A constant is a value provided explicitly by the program and which cannot be changed by the computer during program execution. The 13 could represent a constant hourly rate of pay, i.e., $13 per hour. The -17.2 could be the constant amount to be deducted from a paycheck for insurance and the 3.14159 could be the constant value for pi used in computations. Because of internal limitations within a computer, not all constants may be legally used in BASIC; but the types which may be used permit sufficient scope for the vast majority of problems.

The primary restriction arises because a given computer can retain only a certain number of digits for the representation of a constant. This number will vary from computer to computer but is usually between six and nine. Assuming the number is six, the constant 123456 is legal, whereas 1234567 and -1234567 are not. If you attempt to use an illegal constant, the computer will either send you a message to that effect or simply truncate the constant to a legal size and proceed; so you need not worry about the matter very much at this time.

Note that the constant may be positive or negative. If it is positive, the plus sign may be placed in front of the constant or may be omitted. If it is negative, the minus sign must be placed in front. A decimal point may be present anywhere and may be omitted if it belongs at the right end of the constant—that is, if the constant is an integer. Commas are not permitted: the constant one thousand is written 1000 but not 1,000.

In order to represent very large constants such as one billion or constants very close to zero such as one-billionth, we may use the computer equivalent of scientific notation—that is, we may express a given constant as another constant times the appropriate power of 10. For example, the two constants just mentioned could be written 1.0×10^9 and 1.0×10^{-9} in the usual scientific notation and 1.E9 and 1.E-9 in the computer form. In BASIC the power of 10 is shown by writing E between the first constant and

the second constant, which is the power of 10. There are
of course several ways of representing a given constant in
this scientific (sometimes called "exponential") form: thus
we may write 15000. as 15.E3 or 15E3 or 1.5E4 or .15E5;
similarly we may write .00015 as 15.E-5 or 15E-5 or
1.5E-4. The constant preceding the E may contain up to
the permissible number of digits mentioned above. The
constant following the E, the power of 10, may not be larger
in magnitude than some computer-determined value.

When a computer is executing a program which
happens to generate a constant which is too large, an
"overflow" occurs. Similarly the term "underflow" refers
to a constant which is too small in magnitude for the computer to handle. Usually the computer will type an appropriate message, replace the offending constant with the
largest legal constant in the case of overflow and zero in
the case of underflow, and continue with the program. In
most problems these extremes are seldom encountered,
although an overflow is sometimes seen because of a programming error in which an attempt is made to divide a
constant by zero.

3.3 Variables

A variable is different than a constant in that the value of a
variable changes value during a program. In order to remember the values of various constants which are used in a
program, a computer has a collection of memory cells or
locations which may, for the purpose of writing programs,
be visualized as a set of "mail boxes" into which may be
placed a piece of paper with the value of a constant written
on it—that is, a constant may be stored in a memory
location.

In real life, mail boxes are usually identified by some
name (Mr. J. Jones) or some number (No. 63 or 1498
Columbus Street). Similarly the memory locations in a

computer are identified by certain names which are called "variables." Thus in the program in Chapter 2 when we said LET $X = 25$, we were telling the computer to set aside a memory location which would be named X and to store the constant 25 at that location.

There are three types of variables (memory location names) in most versions of BASIC: simple, subscripted, and string. In this chapter we shall work only with the first, simple variables, which are used to name memory locations holding numerical constants such as those described above.

Although some programming languages, such as FORTRAN, allow an almost unlimited choice of names to be used as variables, BASIC restricts us to variables which consist of either a single letter or a single letter followed by a single digit. Therefore, a variable (memory location) can be represented by any of the 26 letters of the alphabet or by any of these letters in combination with any of the digits 0 to 9. Thus X, B, C1, and N9 are legal variables, but 9N, BX, and X23 are not. We might mention at this point that blanks in BASIC are ignored by the computer (except in messages and string constants which will be discussed later). Consequently the variable X 1 is legal and is the same, from the computer's viewpoint, as X1. In typing programs you are at liberty to use blanks freely to improve the legibility of what you are writing, or you may suppress all of them, a practice we do not recommend.

When writing formulas (see the next section), variables may usually be interpreted and used just as they are in equations. But always keep the above explanation in mind, because there are a few important differences which will become apparent later in the discussion of the replacement statement.

3.4   Formulas

Constants and/or variables combined by the familiar arithmetic operations—for example, $2 + 3$ and $X - 27$—are called "formulas" or "expressions." The formula X—27 says to subtract the constant 27 from the constant which is stored in the memory location whose name is X. We normally just say "subtract 27 from X," but be sure you understand that X itself is *not* a constant but rather is the name of a memory location where a constant is stored.

Addition and subtraction are indicated by the usual symbols + and —. Multiplication is indicated by an asterisk *, division by a slash /, and exponentiation (raising to a power) by an upward arrow ↑. Thus $4*3=12$, $20/5=4$, and $3↑2=9$. Note that if we are multiplying a constant or a variable by another constant or variable, the multiplication sign * must be present even though it is frequently omitted in algebra. Thus the formula to multiply X by 2 must be written $2*X$ or $X*2$ but not $2X$ or even $2(X)$. Neglecting to put in the asterisk is a very common mistake even for experienced programmers; so be on your guard against it. The computer will give a diagnostic message indicating an illegal expression if it encounters such a situation.

A formula may contain several operations. In this event the operations are performed according to certain rules as follows:

1 The formula is scanned from left to right, and any exponentiations are performed in the order in which they are encountered. Thus $2−3↑2/4↑3$ is first reduced to $2−9/4↑3$ and then to $2−9/64$.

2 The resulting formula is again scanned from left to right, and multiplications and divisions are performed in order. Thus $8*4/2*3$ is reduced to $32/2*3$, then to $16*3$, and finally to 48.

3 The resulting formula is again scanned from left to right, and the additions and subtractions are performed in order. Thus $2+3−4+5$ is first reduced to $5−4+5$, then to $1+5$, and finally to 6.

Combining these rules, the formula $2+3*4↑2/6−7$ is first

reduced to $2+3*16/6-7$, then to $2+48/6-7$, then to $2+8-7$, then to $10-7$, and finally to 3.

Pairs of parentheses may be used to modify the order of evaluation of a formula, and a formula may contain several pairs of parentheses, including "nested" pairs in which one pair is inside another pair. The general rule is that the formula within the innermost parentheses pair is first evaluated by the three rules above, the parentheses pair deleted, and this process continued until the entire formula is evaluated. Thus $12/3*2=4*2=8$, but $12/(3*2)=12/6=2$; and $36/(12/(1+3))=36/(12/4)=36/3=12$.

Parentheses may be used even though they are not needed; so if there is any doubt in your mind, use them. Be sure your parentheses occur in pairs, however, as an unpaired parenthesis will be an error and will call forth a diagnostic message from the computer.

A minus sign preceding a variable is treated as a subtraction sign rather than a negation. Hence $-4\uparrow2=-(4\uparrow2)=-16$ rather than $(-4)\uparrow2$ which is $+16$.

3.5 Program Structure

We are now ready to consider how a program is put together. In general a program consists of a series of statements which describe the manipulations which are to take place when the program is executed by the computer. Each statement in the program occupies exactly one line. If you have a statement which would take more than one line to write, you will have to break it up into two or more shorter statements. The maximum length of a line is usually 75 characters including blanks.

Each line of a program must be identified by a line number at the beginning of the line. A line number must be an integer between 1 and 99999 inclusive (9999 for some versions of BASIC). The size of the line number of a statement relative to those of other statements in a program determines when that statement will be used in the execution of the program. The computer will take all the statements of a program as they are typed and arrange them in order according to the sizes of the line numbers. Therefore one does not need to type the program in the order in which it is to be executed. If two statements in a program have the same line number, the first one typed will be replaced by the second. This is a very convenient feature, as it allows us to correct statements at any time and also to insert statements where we wish as we write the program. It is good practice to number the lines in a program by tens rather than by consecutive integers so that there is plenty of room to insert additional statements if needed. You may delete a statement by typing a blank statement having the same line number.

3.6   The END and STØP Statements

The last statement in a program—that is, the statement with the largest line number—must be an END statement, which is written

        535 END

(the line number 535 is for illustrative purposes only). The largest permissible number for your computer is of course always a safe one to use for the END statement. The computer will stop the execution of the program when it reaches this statement in the program.

The computer will also stop execution if the statement

        220 STØP

is encountered. The STØP statement is useful in branching programs, which will be discussed in the next chapter. Note that even if a program contains one or more STØP statements, an END statement is still necessary.

3.7   The Replacement (LET) Statement*

The simple replacement statement is used to initialize a variable (i.e., to place a specific value into a particular variable, as in

100 LET X = 25

This will put the value 25 into variable X. Also the statement is used to place the result of a formula into a particular variable, as in

150 LET Y$=2*3/4$

which will put the constant 1.5 into variable Y.

A formula on the right-hand side of the equals sign may contain variables, but these must have been assigned their proper values in previous statements in the program.

For proper understanding of what it does, the replacement statement

20 LET X$=$Y$+3$

should be read "place into location X the result of adding the constant stored in location Y to the constant 3." This interpretation implies that the equals sign does not necessarily signify equality in the mathematical sense. The statements

10 LET X$=5$
20 LET X$=$X$+16$

are perfectly acceptable in BASIC and will result in the constant 21 being placed in location X when line 20 is executed. The statement in that line says to place into location X the result of adding the constant in X—that is, 5—to the constant 16. So, after statement 20, X has the new value of 21.

---

*In some systems the LET is not necessary, i.e., 100 LET X = 25 can be 100 X = 25

From the above it should be clear that the statement

50 LET 3=X

is nonsense, as 3 is not a legal symbol for a variable. Such a statement will produce a diagnostic.

Be very careful to get the variables in the right order when transferring a constant from one location to another. The statement

30 LET X=Y

copies the constant in location Y into location X. The constant is also retained in Y, but the constant originally in X is lost. On the other hand

30 LET Y=X

does just the opposite.

It is sometimes desirable to put a constant or the result of a formula into several locations. This can be done by using several simple replacement statements, but some versions of BASIC permit it to be accomplished more easily by using the "multiple replacement statement." To put the constant 16 into locations X1, X2, and Y, we could write

50 LET X1=X2=Y=16

which does the same thing as

50 LET X1=16
51 LET X2=16
52 LET Y=16

Note that the exact form of this statement may be different from that given above in different systems.

3.8 The READ, DATA, and RESTØRE Statements

The replacement statement allows us to place a constant into a variable, but its use would clearly become unwieldy if we needed to enter a large number of constants. To overcome this difficulty, we may use the DATA and READ statements.

Say that we wish to place the constants 1, 2, 3, and 4 into the variables A, B, C, and D respectively. We may write the statement

    10 DATA 1,2,3,4

any place in the program. Then the statement

    50 READ A,B,C,D

will place the four constants into the desired locations. We could also have written

    50 READ A
    51 READ B
    52 READ C, D

and the data (the constants) could have been written in several separate statements, such as

    10 DATA 1, 2
    20 DATA 3, 4

In general we may have as many DATA statements in a program as we wish, and they may be located anywhere except after the END statement. The constants listed in each statement are separated by commas, but a comma is not placed before the first or after the last constant. Before executing the program, the computer will search out all DATA statements in the program, place the constants they contain in one long list within the computer in the order in which they occur in the program, and set a "pointer" at the first constant in this combined list. This pointer is internal to the computer and tells the computer which item of data is to be dealt with next. When a READ statement is encountered in the program during execution, the con-

stant at which the pointer is pointing is sent to the location
identified by the first variable in the list following the word
READ. The pointer then moves to the next constant in the
combined list. If another variable is present in the READ
statement (separated by a comma from the first one), the
new constant is sent to that location, the pointer moves to
the next constant, and so on. When another READ statement is encountered, this process is continued. If the
program tries to read more data than is present in the
combined list, execution of the program will stop, and an
appropriate message such as ØUT ØF DATA will be
typed by the computer.

   If you keep a mental, or even a physical, picture of
the combined data list and the pointer in front of you, you
should have little difficulty using these two statements
correctly. For example, consider the program

```
10 DATA 3.1E−10
20 READ A
30 READ B
40 DATA 17
50 END
```

To understand the execution of the program, first write
down the combined data list and attach a pointer at the
first entry:

```
3.1E−10, 17
   ↑
```

Then write down the variables occurring in the program:

```
A:
B:
```

As constants are assigned to the variables by the program,
write them down. The execution of line 20 consists of
placing the constant $3.1E − 10$ into location A and moving
the pointer one place to the right.

3.1E − 10, 17
↑
A: 3.1E − 10
B:

Similarly after line 30 has been executed, we have

3.1E − 10, 17
↑
A: 3.1E − 10
B: 17

Notice that the pointer has now moved beyond the data, and if we added the statement

45 READ C

to the program, we would get an ØUT ØF DATA message when the computer attempted to execute line 45.

It may happen that you need to read the same data more than once within a program. This can be done by using the statement

100 RESTØRE

which moves the pointer back to the beginning of the combined data list. The statement may be used regardless of where the pointer is located. For example, the program

10 DATA 16, −2
20 READ A,B
30 RESTØRE
40 READ C,D
50 END

will assign the constant 16 to variables A and C and the constant −2 to variables B and D.

3.9 The PRINT Statement

We have seen how to get constants into the computer and how to do certain arithmetic operations on those constants. Now we need to learn how to get the answers from the computer. This is done by using a PRINT statement.

The PRINT statement consists of the word PRINT followed by a list of what is to be printed. The statement

```
40 PRINT A,B
```

will cause the computer to print on the terminal the constants stored in locations A and B.

Besides variables, the print list may include formulas, constants, and messages. If a formula is written in the list, the computer will evaluate it and print the result (as in the program in Chapter 2). A "message" is any set of symbols which is enclosed between two quotation marks. (Some systems use the apostrophe in place of the quotation mark.) For example,

```
10 LET X=5
20 PRINT "X=", X, "X PLUS 2=", X+2
```

will give the printout

```
X=      5     X PLUS 2=   7
```

The manner in which the items to be printed are arranged on the paper is called the "print format." We will defer until a later chapter the consideration of the ways of getting a desired format and will describe here what is called the "standard" print format.

In most versions of BASIC this format considers the print line to be 75 spaces long and divides the line into five parts or "fields" of 15 spaces each. The items in a print list (separated by commas) are then printed one to a field in consecutive fields. If more than five fields are needed for one PRINT statement, the printer goes to the next line or lines on the paper as required.

Normally the printout will start on a new line each time a PRINT statement is encountered in the program. To have the printout from two consecutive PRINT statements occur on the same line, put a comma after the last item in the print list of the first statement. This technique can be applied to several PRINT statements if desired. Thus

```
10 PRINT "JØE"
20 PRINT "MABEL"
```

will produce the printout

```
JØE
MABEL
```

but changing line 10 to

```
10 PRINT "JØE",
```

will give

```
JØE    MABEL
```

A PRINT statement with no list following it will cause the printer to skip one line and is used to separate lines of output data if desired.

Different versions of BASIC will print different numbers of significant digits, and the rules for the manner in which constants are printed are quite involved. For the beginner it is really not a matter of major importance, and we suggest you avoid the details until you gain a little experience and are ready to become concerned about such problems. At that time consultation with the manual for your BASIC and some experimentation will set you straight.

3.10   The REM Statement

It is occasionally desirable, particularly in a long and complicated program, to insert remarks within the body of the program to remind you of what is happening or for clarity. This can be done by using the REM statement:

```
10 REM THIS PRØGRAM WAS WRITTEN
20 REM BY G. G. BITTER
```

The message following the word REM is ignored by the computer when executing the program but will be included when a listing is requested. This statement, like all others, requires a line number.

3.11   Debugging

It seems almost inevitable that a program will not work the first time it is tried—although one always hopes. To increase the chances for success or to run down errors when the first trial is not successful, it is a good practice to go through the program step by step, pretending you are the computer. Write on a piece of paper all of the variables in the program and the combined data list if there is one. Then start through the program, changing the values in the variables as directed by the program. Be sure to do exactly what the program says to do, *not* what you would like it to do. This process will help you to understand what happens in the computer and will usually find logical errors in the program. It will be particularly useful in the more complicated programs you will write later.

Also scan your program both before and during the typing of it on the terminal to check for spelling and punctuation errors and incorrect forms for the BASIC statements. A minor misspelling or omission of an occasional comma seldom interferes much when one is writing instructions to a rational human being, but you must never forget that when writing programs for a computer you are attempting to communicate with a thoroughly unimaginative machine.

Most computers actually handle programs in two steps after being given the RUN command. In the first step, called "compilation," the BASIC program is translated to another language—machine language. During the compilation process grammatical errors in the program are looked for. If any are found, diagnostic messages are sent to you. These messages will tell you approximately what is wrong and the line numbers of the statements where the errors occurred. The BASIC manual for your computer should include a list of the various error messages (diagnostics) and their meanings. (Some computers do the initial diagnosis line-by-line as the program is typed.)

When you receive an error message, take a quick look to see if the mistake is obvious. If it is, correct it by retyping the offending line or lines and try again. If the trouble is not apparent and needs some further thought, save in the computer what you have done by typing the system command SAVE. The computer will store the current version of your program under the name that you gave it. When the computer indicates it has done this, sign off in the usual way, and then you may think at your leisure. When you have found the trouble, dial the computer and call for the old problem with whatever name you used. Make the necessary corrections by typing the proper lines and proceed. If you still have problems, another SAVE or a REPLACE command (see Appendix D) will replace the old saved program with the latest version. If you have to go through this procedure very often with one program or have to make many corrections, it is wise to have the computer list the program occasionally to see just what the latest version is.

If you do save a program within the computer, be

sure to unsave it when you are through with it. Otherwise it will remain in the computer's files indefinitely.

When the computer has been able to compile your program, it goes to the second step and attempts to execute it. There may be some execution errors for which you will receive messages; or possibly everything will seem to work all right, except the answers will be wrong, which implies there are logical errors in the program. In either case you will make corrections on the spot if they are obvious or save the program and think about it.

It is worth mentioning that if you write a complicated program, it should always be tried out with some simple check cases to determine whether or not the program is producing correct answers. If the answers are incorrect, don't blame the computer. Computers very seldom make mistakes, which is more than can be said about even the best programmers.

There is of course a slight chance the program will compile and execute correctly the first time. If so, congratulations!

3.12 Questions

Answers appear at the end of the question set.

1 Consider the following program:

```
10 LET 2=X
20 LET Y=X
30 LET Z=(X*(Y+2.4)
40 PRIMT X,Y,"Z=",Z
50 EN D
```

a Go through the program and correct each line if necessary.

b After the program has been corrected, what value will be stored in Z before line 30 has been executed?

c What value will be stored in Z after line 30 has been executed?

d What will the printout be?

2 Consider the following program:

```
10 DATA 4, − 1,7
20 READ A
30 LET C=2↑(2+A)
40 READ A
50 PRINT A,C
60 END
```

a What constant will be stored in A after line 20 has been executed?

b What constant will be stored in A after line 40 has been executed?

c What constant will be stored in C after line 30 has been executed?

d What line number(s) other than 10 could be given to the DATA statement?

3 What value will be stored in X by each of the following formulas?

a LET X=3↑3↑3

b LET X=(3↑3↑3)

c LET X=(3↑3)↑3

d LET X=3↑(3↑3)

4 In grade school we would refer to 3/4 as a number. What is it in BASIC?

5 Which of the following are not legal variables:
M, ME, M1, M0, M11, 2M?

6 Which of the following sets of statements will
interchange the constants stored in locations X
and Y (in an actual program the statements
would of course be on separate lines and have
line numbers)?

(1) LET V=X; LET X=Y; LET Y=V
(2) LET X=Y; LET Y=X
(3) LET V=X; LET Y=V; LET X=Y

7 What would be the printout of the following
program?

10 LET M=4
20 PRINT "M=",M,M+3
30 END

8 Consider the following program:

10 PRINT "STUDENT"
20 PRINT "PØWER"
30 END

a What will the printout be?

b If we changed line 10 to

10 PRINT "STUDENT",

what will the printout be?

9 What will the following statement do?

50 PRINT

10 What will the printout of the following program
be?

10 DATA 3,2,5,19,32
20 READ A,B,C

```
30 LET P=(A+B)↑2/C
50 READ P, A
60 PRINT P,A,B,C
70 END
```

3.13 Answers

1 *a* Line 10 is nonsense, as 2 is not a legal variable. Presumably the statement should be 10 LET X=2. Line 20 is O.K. and will assign the value of X (which is 2) to Y. In the formula in line 30 there are two left parentheses but only one on the right. Actually the first left parenthesis is superfluous; so you may either delete it or add a right mate between the X and the * or at the right-hand end of the formula. In line 40 the word PRINT is misspelled. Although EN D looks peculiar in line 50, the computer will ignore the blank.

  b Either 0 (which is automatically assigned to all variables before execution starts in some versions of BASIC) or whatever was left over from the previous program.

  c As X and Y are each equal to 2, Z=2*(2+2.4) =2*4.4=8.8

  d 2   2   Z=   8.8

2 *a* 4, the first element in the combined data list.

  b −1, the second element in the data list.

  c As A=4 at that point, C=2↑(2+4)=2↑6=64.

  d Any integer between 1 and 59 inclusive except 10, 20, 30, 40, or 50, because the position of DATA statements within a program is immaterial.

3 a 3↑3↑3 = 27↑3 = 19683.

  b 19683; the parentheses have no effect here.

  c Again 19683, as the parentheses do not alter the normal order of operation.

  d 3↑27 = 7.6256E12.

4 3/4 is a formula which produces the constant .75.

5 ME, M11, and 2M are illegal.

6 (1) is the only correct one. Assume X=2 and Y=3; then if (1) is executed, X=3 and Y=2; if (2) is executed, X=3 and Y=3; if (3) is executed, X=2 and Y=2.

7 M=   4   7

8 a STUDENT
    PØWER

  b STUDENT   PØWER

9 Skip a line in the printout.

10 19   32   2   5

3.14 Exercises

1 Write and run a program to do the following:

  a Read from a data list the three numbers 5, 7, and 2 and put them into locations A, B, and C respectively.

  b Compute the sum of the three numbers and place it into location S.

  c Compute the product of the three numbers and place it into location P.

d Print as follows:
  First line: the values of A, B, and C
  Second line: blank
  Third line: the message "S=" followed by the
  value of S
  Fourth line: the message "P=" followed by the
  value of P

2 Write and run a program to do the following:

a Read in a number of half dollars, quarters,
  dimes, nickels, and pennies.

b Compute the total amount of money.

c Print the number of half dollars, quarters,
  dimes, nickels, and pennies as well as the total
  amount of money.

BASIC
control statements

4.1 Introduction

The three BASIC statements that will be discussed in this chapter open the door for programming some very sophisticated problems and are indispensable. Fortunately, they are fairly simple to understand and use. We will also introduce the concept of a "flowchart," which is a picture of the logical flow of information and action within a program.

4.2 Flowcharts

A flowchart is a diagram of the operations which are to take place in a program. Such a chart can be a great help in understanding the logical structure of a complicated problem, and we will occasionally make use of one to describe a problem in this book.

Although a large number of different symbols may be, and frequently are, used in flowcharts, we will restrict ourselves to four: ovals, to indicate starting and stopping points; diamonds, to indicate questions (and consequently branch points); rectangles, to indicate arithmetic and replacement operations; parallelograms, to indicate input/output operations such as reading and printing; and arrows for flowchart direction. Examples of these symbols are shown in Figure 4.1.

Reading a flowchart is important if you are to know how to apply one to help you logically set up a computer program. See if you can follow the example.

The flowchart in Figure 4.2 computed the pay for a week. If the number of hours was 40 hours or less the directions were to multiply the number of hours by $14 and print the total pay. If the number of hours was over 40 then the directions were to multiply hours over 40 by $20 and add this to the 40 hours at the $14 rate and print the total pay.

As can be seen, the flowchart is a very convenient way to organize thoughts and prepare a problem to be pro-

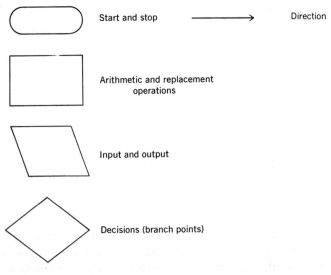

FIGURE 4.1 **Flowchart Symbols**

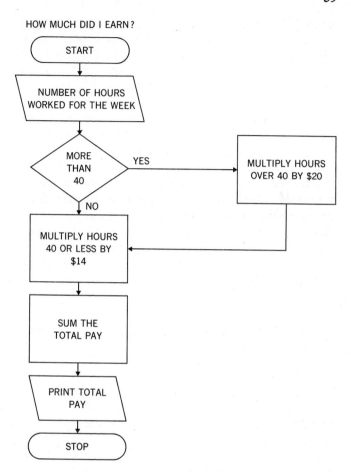

FIGURE 4.2 **How Much Did I Earn Flowchart**

grammed. We do not have a strong opinion about the desirability of drawing a flowchart for every problem but simply observe that in some cases they can help immensely in deciding what, when, and how to do certain things. In any event, try your hand at one or two just to get a feeling for them and to get sufficiently acquainted so that you will be able to read one intelligently. It is of course not necessary to put everything into a flowchart, and often a "bare bones" diagram will serve quite as well as one complete in every detail.

4.3 Relations

The IF-THEN statement, which will be introduced in the next section, allows us to do different things or to choose alternative courses of action, depending upon the relative sizes of two constants. BASIC allows us to ask six different questions about this relative size or relationship. The six relation symbols and their meanings are:

$=$ is equal to
$<$ is less than
$>$ is greater than
$<=$ is less than or equal to
$>=$ is greater than or equal to
$<>$ is not equal to

The first three symbols are the same as those used in high school algebra. The last three are similar to the usual ones and differ from them only because of the limitations of the terminal keyboard. When typing these last three, be careful to use the correct order. For example, you may not use $=<$ in place of $<=$.

4.4 The IF-THEN Statement

The following is a typical IF-THEN statement:

40 IF X$<$13 THEN 100

In words this statement says, "If the constant stored in

location X is less than 13, then branch to line 100—that is, execute next the statement at line 100; otherwise move on to the next statement after line 40." Because of its action, this statement is sometimes called a "branching" statement.

Consider the program:

```
10 LET N=97
20 IF N>100 THEN 50
30 PRINT N, "IS NØT GREATER THAN 100"
40 STOP
50 PRINT N, "IS GREATER THAN 100"
60 END
```

As it stands, the value of N at line 20 is 97. Consequently the question "Is N greater than 100?" is answered in the negative; the program moves on to the next statement in sequence at line 30 where the printout

97   IS NØT GREATER THAN 100

occurs; and the program then stops as instructed by line 40. If we change line 10 to

10 LET N=105

the question in the IF-THEN statement is answered affirmatively; the program branches to line 50 where the printout

105   IS GREATER THAN 100

occurs; and the program stops because the END statement has been reached.

You may ask about a relationship between two constants (which would not be a very interesting question), two variables, a variable and a constant (as in the program above), or, most generally, two formulas. The statement

500 IF A*E↑2<>47.36−X/(93+Y) THEN 200

is perfectly permissible. Note carefully that there is *not* a comma before the word THEN. If you put one there, a diagnostic will be given.

Also note that control may be directed back to an earlier part of the program—that is, the line number following THEN may be smaller than the line number of the IF-THEN statement. This is frequently very useful but does open up the possibility of an "infinite loop." Consider the program:

```
10 LET X=2
20 LET Y=2
30 IF X=Y THEN 10
40 END
```

The END statement in this program will never be reached, and the computer will spend the rest of its days (or until the proper system command is given to stop it) asking if 2 equals 2. It is unlikely that even a novice would write and try to run this program, but in more complicated programs infinite loops may occur inadvertently. Watch out for them!

About the only way to know if the computer is in an infinite loop is to observe that it is taking much too long to execute the program. The programs you write for this manual should seldom take over five seconds to run. If the time goes much beyond that—say, twenty or thirty seconds—stop the execution (in most systems by the BREAK key on the terminal). When processing has stopped, push the BRK-RLS button, which will have lighted up when the BREAK key was depressed. If this does not stop program execution, check your system manual for terminating execution details. You may then check your suspicions by inserting a PRINT statement of some kind into the middle of what might be an infinite loop and see what happens (although it would be preferable to save the program and think awhile first). For example, in the program above we could insert

25 PRINT "I AM AT LINE 25"

and the message would be printed each time the loop was executed. After a few dozen such messages appeared, it would be clear what was happening.

There may be times when it is desirable to stop the execution of a program, even if everything is apparently going along all right; so be sure to learn how to do so on your system. On some systems, pushing the CLEAR button will turn everything off.

4.5   The GØ TØ Statement

After a program has branched to a certain place with an IF-THEN statement and the necessary operations have been performed, you may wish to have it jump somewhere else without asking any more questions. This can be done by using

170 GØ TØ 340

which will unconditionally direct the computer to the statement at line 340.

You should verify that line 40 in the first program in the last section could be replaced by

40 GØ TØ 60

without affecting the operation of the program. This means that the STØP statement is really superfluous, as it can always be replaced by a GØ TØ statement directing the program to the END statement. Nevertheless the STØP statement is convenient to use at times and should remain a part of your BASIC vocabulary.

The program below illustrates the combined use of the IF-THEN and GØ TØ statements. The purpose of the program is to determine whether the constant stored in location X is positive, negative, or zero. The value of X is assigned in statement 10. See if you can understand the program operation before reading the explanation below.

```
10 LET X = -7.6
20 IF X<0 THEN 60
30 IF X=0 THEN 80
40 PRINT X, "IS PØSITIVE"
50 GØ TØ 90
60 PRINT X, "IS NEGATIVE"
70 GØ TØ 90
80 PRINT X, "IS ZERØ"
90 END
```

Line 20 asks if X is negative. If the answer is "yes," the program branches to line 60 where the value of X and the message "IS NEGATIVE" are printed, followed by a jump to line 90. If the answer is "no," the program goes on to the next line (line 30), which then asks if X is zero. If the answer there is "yes," the program branches to line 80, prints the appropriate information, and jumps to line 90. If the answer is "no," the program moves on to the next line in sequence (line 40). As X must be either negative, zero, or positive, an IF-THEN statement to check for positiveness is not needed, as checks for the first two alternatives have already been made; therefore the appropriate information is printed and a jump made to line 90.

4.6 Counters

The program below introduces the concept of a "counter" variable, which serves to count the number of times a certain event occurs as the program is executed. As you will see in the next chapter, such variables are extremely important and occur in almost every computer program. In general we need counters for two purposes: first, to make a count of events in order to report the total number of occurrences (like a gatekeeper at a football game, who will report the total daily attendance); and, second, to keep track of the number of times an event has occurred so that some action may be taken when the count reaches a certain value (not unlike an elevator "starter," who must not allow more than a certain number of people to get on an elevator).

The replacement statement LET $X = X + 1$ is often used as a counter. Each time this statement is executed it increases or increments by one. The following program

```
10 LET X=0
20 LET X=X+1
30 PRINT X
40 IF X=10 THEN 60
50 GO TO 20
60 END
```

will produce the following output.

```
1
2
3
4
5
6
7
8
9
10
```

As can be seen each time the counter is executed it increases by one, i.e., X is replaced by the value $X + 1$ or if $X = 2$ then $X = 2 + 1$ or the new value of X is 3, etc.

The more interesting program on the next page counts separately the number of times negative, zero, and positive constants appear in a data list.

In this program four counters are used: three of them (N, Z, and P) count the number of negative, zero, and positive constants respectively for reporting purposes; the fourth (T) counts the number of constants tested so that the computer will know when it is through. The first DATA statement contains one constant whose value is the number of constants to be checked. The constants themselves are given in the second DATA statement (line 20). The two DATA statements could of course be combined into one but are separated here for the sake of clarity, a feature which is to be encouraged in program writing.

```
 10 DATA 8
 20 DATA 7,−6,−43,0,3,−29,0,5280
 30 LET N=0
 40 LET Z=0
 50 LET P=0
 60 LET T=0
 70 READ A
 80 READ X
 90 IF X<0 THEN 130
100 IF X=0 THEN 150
110 LET P=P+1 ← Counts positive numbers
120 GØ TØ 160
130 LET N=N+1 ← Counts negative numbers
140 GØ TØ 160
150 LET Z=Z+1 ← Counts number of zeros
160 LET T = T + 1 ← Counts total number
                      of numbers checked.
170 IF T<A THEN 80
180 PRINT N,Z,P
190 END
```

The four counters are assigned initial values of zero in lines 30, 40, 50, and 60. (Some versions of BASIC automatically assign zero to *every* variable in a program before starting execution, but some do not; we recommend explicit initialization of counter variables so that there is no possibility of an error and to emphasize the program logic.) Line 70 reads the number of constants to be tested and places the number into A. Line 80 reads the first constant to be tested and places it into X. Line 90 determines whether the constant is negative or not. If it is, a branch is made to line 130, where the negative counter is incremented by one. If it is not, the program moves on to line 100, where a check for the constant being zero is made. If the constant is zero, a branch is made to line 150, where the zero counter is incremented by one. If it is not zero, it must be positive, and line 110 increments the positive counter by one (we are using the fact that any constant must be either negative, zero, or positive). After the appropriate counter has been incremented, the program goes to line 160, where the counter T is incremented by one. Line 170 then checks to see if all the constants have been tested. If not, the program branches back to line 80, where the next constant is read, but otherwise the final values of N, Z, and P are printed in line 180 (3, 2, and 3 respectively with the given data), and the program ends.

We strongly recommend your making a thorough analysis of the program, including the combined data list and all program variables.

It should be noted that the program could be shortened somewhat by using the fact that the sum of N, Z, and P at line 180 must be T, and consequently it is not necessary actually to keep track of all three of them. For example, we could replace the statement in line 110 by GØ TØ 160, delete lines 50 and 120, and replace the statement in line 180 by PRINT N,Z,T−N−Z. An alternative simplification would be to use the fact that the sum of N, Z, and P is always equal to T at line 170. Thus we could delete lines 60 and 160, change the GØ TØ 160 statement to GØ TØ 170, and change the statement in line 170 to IF $N+Z+P<A$ THEN 80. Such simplifications are marks of "cleverness" on the part of the programmer, and we encourage you to

look for such possibilities in the programs which you write. There is the ever-present danger of becoming so clever that you outwit yourself, so be a little careful; and if there is any serious doubt, take the straightforward approach.

4.7   The ØN-GØ TØ Statement

The GØ TØ statement discussed in Section 4.5 is sometimes called an "unconditional" GØ TØ because there are no conditions which might permit an alternative action. Many versions of BASIC contain a conditional type of branching statement, the ØN-GØ TØ statement. This has the form:

$$40 \text{ ØN X GØ TØ } 70,100,30$$

This multiple branching statement will direct the computer to line 70 if the value of X is 1, to line 100 if X is 2, and to line 30 if X is 3. If the value of X is, say, 2.8, the number will be truncated (*not* rounded) to 2, and the branch will be made to line 100.

In place of a simple variable (X in the example) any formula may be used. When the statement is being executed, the value of the formula will be computed and, if not an integer, truncated. There may be any number of line numbers in the list following TØ: the first goes with the value 1 of the control variable or formula, the second with 2, etc. If the value of the control variable or formula is negative, zero, or greater than the number of line numbers in the list, a diagnostic will be typed and execution of the program stopped. The same line number may appear more than once in the list.

If your BASIC allows this statement, it can be very useful in certain situations, although one can get along without it because it can be replaced by a series of IF-THEN statements. For example, assuming X is some integer, the statement above could be replaced by

```
40 IF X=1 THEN 70
41 IF X=2 THEN 100
42 IF X=3 THEN 30
43 PRINT "CØNTRØL INTEGER ØUT ØF RANGE"
44 STØP
```

If X is not an integer, it would be necessary to truncate its value in order to simulate the ØN–GØ TØ statement completely. This requires the use of the INT library function, to be discussed in a later chapter.

We might stress at this time the fact that there are usually many ways of writing a program to perform certain tasks. For you, a beginning student, it is important to write programs which are clear and understandable, even though they may be much longer than absolutely necessary. As you gain experience, knowledge, and confidence, you will learn to become clever in minimizing the sizes of your programs by various tricks or subtleties. But always keep in mind the hard-won maxim that the simplest and most straightforward approach almost always is the fastest and safest.

4.8   Using Flowcharts

Flowcharts for the program in section 4.6 for counting the number of negative, zero, and positive constants are shown in Figures 4.3 and 4.4. The first is a general flowchart which could be used by a programmer working in any computer language, while the second is somewhat more specific.

As a further example of how a flowchart may be used to display the logic involved in a problem, consider the following: we wish to write a program to compute the

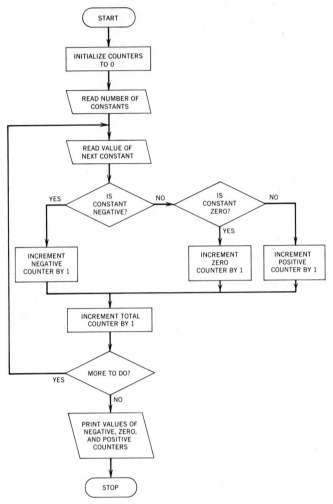

FIGURE 4.3 **General Negative-Zero-Positive Problem Flowchart**

take-home pay for several employees. The take-home pay
for an individual is his/her gross pay reduced for insurance
purposes by 1 percent for each dependent and also reduced
by $10 if he/she belongs to the Santa Claus Club. For each

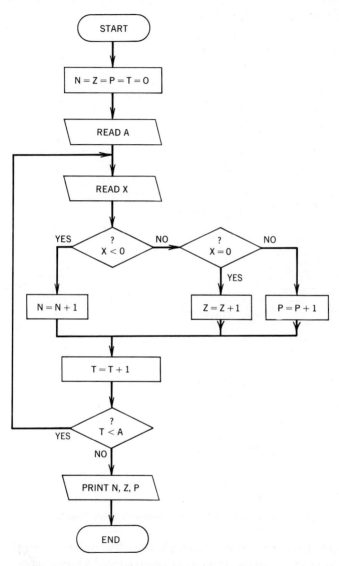

FIGURE 4.4 **Specific Negative-Zero-Positive Flowchart**

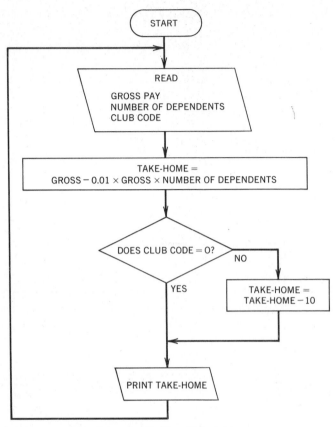

FIGURE 4.5 **Take-home Pay Problem Flowchart**

employee the supplied data will be (in this order) his/her gross pay, the number of dependents, and a constant indicating whether or not he/she belongs to the Santa Claus Club (1 if he/she does, 0 if he/she doesn't). A flowchart for the problem is shown in Figure 4.5. Study it carefully and convince yourself that the program below reproduces the logical steps shown in the flowchart. The program reads, processes, and prints the results for each employee one at a time until the data are exhausted, at which time the computer will type an "ØUT ØF DATA" message and stop. The data given are for two employees.

```
10 READ G,N,C
20 LET T=G−.01*N*G
30 IF C=0 THEN 50
40 LET T=T−10
50 PRINT T
60 GØ TØ 10
70 DATA 100,3,0,150,2,1
80 END
```

One could use an ØN-GØ TØ statement by replacing line 30 with

```
30 ØN C+1 GØ TØ 50,40
```

although there would normally be little point in doing so when there are only two possibilities at a decision point such as this one.

Flowcharts are of particular value for documenting a program which is to be retained and used at a later date by either the original programmer or others. It is frequently a very difficult chore to unravel the logical complexities in a program as written for a computer, whereas a carefully drawn flowchart will usually indicate very clearly just what is being done. Even if you don't draw a flowchart before writing a program, do so afterwards if you plan to keep it. The flowchart will save many inconveniences in the future.

4.9 Questions

1 Assume $A=12$ and $B=4$. Each part below contains an IF-THEN statement with line number 50. Assume the next statement in sequence is line

number 60. For each part give the line number of the statement to which the program will branch as a result of the IF-THEN statement.

a 50 IF A>B THEN 100
b 50 IF A−3*B<0 THEN 100
c 50 IF A/3=B THEN 100
d 50 IF A+B<=B↑2 THEN 100
e 50 IF A−B>=B*B THEN 100
f 50 IF A/B<>B−1 THEN 100

2 Given the statement

50 ØN N/M GØ TØ 30,80,70,5280

what will the program do if

a N=8 and M=3?

b N=20 and M=4?

c N=4 and M=−4?

3 Consider the following program:

```
100 READ X
110 DATA, 5
120 IF X>=16, THEN 160
130 DATA 7,18,3
140 PRINT X,
150 GØ TØ 100
```

a Debug the program—that is, make any necessary corrections.

b What will the printout be after the corrections are made?

c What will the printout be if line 130 is replaced by 130 DATA 7,8,3?

d What would happen to the printout if the comma after the X in line 140 were deleted?

4.10 Answers

1 *a* 100, as 12 is greater than 4.

   b 60, as $12-3*4=12-12=0$, which is not less than 0.

   c 100, as $12/3=4$.

   d 100, as $12+4=16$ and equals (and so is less than or equal to) $4\uparrow2$.

   e 60, as $12-4=8$, which is not greater than or equal to $4*4=16$.

   f 60, as $12/4$ equals $4-1$.

2 *a* Branch to line 80, as $8/3$ will be truncated to 2.

   b A diagnostic will be given, and the program will stop, because $20/4=5$, and there are only four line numbers following the GØ TØ.

   c A diagnostic will be given, and the program will stop, because $4/(-4)=-1$.

3 *a* In line 110 there should not be a comma after the word DATA. In line 120 there should not be a comma before the word THEN. There is no END statement (the END statement must have a line number 160 to satisfy the branch in line 120).

   b 5   7
   c 5   7   8   3

   followed by an "ØUT ØF DATA" message.

   d The numbers would appear one on a line rather than all on one line.

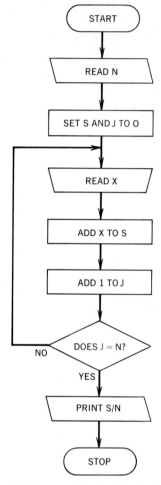

FIGURE 4.6   **Exercise Problem Flowchart**

4.11   Exercises

1   Write and run a program to do the operations
shown in the flowchart in Figure 4.6. The problem
is to compute the arithmetic average of N num-

bers and print the result. The value of N and the N numbers are to be given in one DATA statement. For your program use the following data list:

7,14.2,9.3,10.0,15.9,6.2,7.8,13.5

The constant 7, the first number in the list, is the value of N.

In the flowchart the variable J is used as a counter to tell how many of the N numbers have been processed and hence to determine when the entire list has been finished. The variable S contains the sum of the numbers and is incremented each time a new number is processed. Note that both J and S are to be initialized to zero at the beginning of the program.

2 Write and run a program to print the numbers 1 to 100 including the square and cube of each. Label as follows:

```
        NUMBER =
SQUARE OF THE NUMBER =
 CUBE OF THE NUMBER =
```

5

loops and arrays

5.1 · Introduction

The uses of the IF-THEN statement lead to a great economy in some programs by permitting the programmer to repeat certain operations without writing statements for each repetition. This procedure, called "looping," is used in a large majority of digital computer programs and is a vital part of the beginning student's programming toolbox. For example, a program to find the sum of the first 1,000 positive integers would be very laborious to write unless looping were used (or unless one happened to know the simple formula for giving the answer immediately). With looping, the program becomes very easy. Take a few minutes and try to write one before looking at the version given in the next section.

Although the IF-THEN statement together with the GØ TØ can adequately handle even the most complicated looping situation, it is more convenient to have statements designed explicitly for this purpose. In this chapter we will discuss such a statement, the FØR-TØ statement and its ever-present shadow, the NEXT statement. Also arrays and subscripted variables, whose effective use goes hand in hand with loops, will be introduced.

5.2 Loops

The program below, which adds the first 1,000 positive integers, shows the use of the IF-THEN statement in a simple loop. Study it carefully and be sure you understand its operation.

```
10 LET S=0
20 LET N=1
30 LET S=S+N
40 LET N=N+1
50 IF N<=1000 THEN 30
60 PRINT S
70 END
```

In this program the variable N is used in a dual capacity: first, it serves as a counter (or "index") to keep track of how many times the loop has been executed; and second, its value is actually used in the arithmetic operation in line 30. The loop itself consists of lines 30, 40, and 50. In many programs the counter is used only for counting; but in others, such as this one, it may be used for other purposes as well. The variable S contains the required sum. Note that S is initialized to zero and N is initialized to 1 before the loop is started.

In general any loop must contain these features: before the loop is begun, a counter is assigned some initial value (line 20); at some point within the loop the counter is incremented by some quantity, the step size (line 40); and finally the value of the counter is compared with some terminal or final value to determine if the looping should be continued or not (line 50).

5.3   The FØR-TØ and NEXT Statements

Using the FØR-TØ and NEXT statements, the program in the previous section can be written

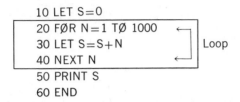

```
10 LET S=0
20 FØR N=1 TØ 1000      ←⌐
30 LET S=S+N                │  Loop
40 NEXT N               ←⌐
50 PRINT S
60 END
```

These are the actions of the FØR-TØ and NEXT statements in this program. When the program reaches line 20, the counter N is assigned the initial value of 1. The program proceeds as usual; and when the NEXT statement is encountered at line 40, N is increased by 1. The new value of the counter is compared with the final value of 1000; if the new value of the counter does not exceed the final value, the loop, starting at the first statement following the FØR-TØ statement, is executed again; otherwise the program branches to the first statement following the NEXT.

Note that the counter variable and the initial and final values are given in the FØR-TØ statement, and this statement begins the loop. The loop is terminated by the NEXT statement. Also note that in this program the step size is not mentioned explicitly; it could be stated by replacing line 20 by

```
20 FØR N=1 TØ 1000 STEP 1
```

To simplify the understanding of FØR-TØ NEXT statements a step-by-step explanation of the first four loops in the above program is as follows:

```
LOOP 1
  N=1
  S=S+N=0+1
  or S=1
```

```
LOOP 2
  N = 2
  S = S + N = 1 + 2
  or S = 3
LOOP 3
  N = 3
  S = S + N = 3 + 3
  or S = 6
LOOP 4
  N = 4
  S = S + N = 6 + 4
  or S = 10
    ETC . . .
```

The vast majority of loops use a step size of 1, and it is perfectly acceptable to omit the "STEP 1" from the FØR-TØ statement in such cases.

As an example of a program in which a step size other than 1 is useful, change line 20 in the program to

```
20 FØR N = 1 TØ 1000 STEP 2
```

The counter will now take on the values of 1, 3, 5,...,999, and the program will find the sum of the odd positive integers between 1 and 999 inclusive. The final value in the FØR-TØ statement could be changed from 1000 to 999, but it is not necessary to do so, because when the counter has reached 999, its next possible value is 1001, which is greater than 1000 and will cause the termination of the looping.

In a FØR-TØ statement the counter must always be a variable; but the initial value, final value, and step size may be constants, variables, or formulas (which will be evaluated by the computer when the loop is first entered).

The initial and final values and the step size may also be negative and/or nonintegers. By using negative values, it is possible to get into an infinite loop, and extra care should be taken in this case. For example, the FØR-TØ statement in the above program could have been written

20 FØR N=1000 TØ 1 STEP −1

which would give the same result as before, but writing

20 FØR N=1 TØ 1000 STEP −1

would produce an infinite loop, as N would never exceed the final value of 1000.

Several FØR-TØ loops may be used within a program. They may follow one another, or there may be loops within loops within loops, etc. (nested loops). However, overlapping loops are *not* permitted. If two or more loops are nested, they must have different counter variables and consequently separate NEXT statements, because a NEXT statement explicitly mentions the counter variable. For example, the following partial program which shows two nested loops is permissible (. . . indicates other statements within the program):

```
    . . .
  FØR M=1 TØ 10
    . . .
  ┌──────────────────────────────┐
  │ FØR J=12 TØ 138 STEP 3        │
  │ . . .                         │
  │ NEXT J                        │
  └──────────────────────────────┘
    . . .
  NEXT M
    . . .
```

The program on the top of page 83, showing two overlapping loops, is *not* permissible and would generate a diagnostic message.

If the initial value is greater than the terminating value and the step size is positive, the loop is skipped over entirely in most versions of BASIC, but some dialects force the loop to be executed at least once. This suggests that

```
    . . .
  FØR M=1 TØ 10
    . . .
    FØR J=12 TØ 138 STEP 3
      . . .
    NEXT M
    . . .
  NEXT J
    . . .
```

with some systems the description of the action of a FØR-TØ loop given earlier may not be completely accurate. However, the description and the actual behavior differ only in minor details at most, and it is unlikely that you will be led astray by any discrepancies.

When a FØR-TØ loop is completed, the counter will retain the value it had during the last time through the loop, and that value may be used later on in the program if needed. Also the counter variable itself may be used for another loop or other purposes once the original loop is completed.

The value of the counter may be changed within the loop, but normally this is not done, since it can easily produce difficulties. For example, the following statements produce an infinite loop, as J will always have the value 0 when line 70 is reached:

```
50 FØR J=1 TØ 5
60 LET J=J−1
70 NEXT J
```

5.4 Arrays and Subscripted Variables

It may have occurred to you that using a loop might be very helpful in reading or printing a long list of data. If this idea is followed through, it will be found that the variable symbols we have used up to now make such a scheme unworkable because it would be necessary to change the variable names with each repetition of the loop. In almost all branches of mathematics when many variables must be manipulated within a single problem, one frequently makes use of "subscripted" variables; and the same idea has been incorporated into BASIC.

If you have not used subscripted variables before, they may give a little trouble at first. Remember, however, that they were invented to save both mental and physical effort, and their use is indispensable in many computer programs.

Subscripted variables are normally written as X_1 (X sub-one), A_{16} (A sub-sixteen), and so forth. Because of the difficulty of printing one symbol slightly below another on a single line when using terminals and other printing devices that may normally be attached to a computer, for computer programs the subscript is written in parentheses following the variable rather than on a lower level. Consequently X_1 is written X(1) and A_{16} is written A(16).

To distinguish subscripted variables from the type we have been using until now, we will refer to the latter as "simple" variables whenever the distinction is necessary. Be careful not to confuse a simple variable such as Y2 with Y(2), which is subscripted variable.

In BASIC there are two types of subscripted variables: singly subscripted and doubly subscripted. Their meanings are easily explained by the following analogy if you keep in mind that *any* variable, single or subscripted, is just the name of a storage location in the memory of the computer. Assume we live in a town which contains several houses, several motels, and several hotels. To send a letter to someone living in one of the houses, it is sufficient to give just the name of the house; this corresponds to the use of a simple variable such as X or B5. To send a letter to a person living in a motel, we must give both the name of the motel and the room number; this corresponds to the use of a singly subscripted variable. Therefore, D(3) might refer to room 3 in motel D. Finally to send a letter to a resident of a hotel we give the hotel name, the floor number, and the room number on that floor; this corresponds to the use of a doubly subscripted variable. The variable $N(27,4)$ might then refer to room 27 on the fourth floor of hotel N (we realize most hotels do not actually work this way but trust you will permit us to stretch a point as this *is* the way in which computer "hotels" operate).

The analogy suggests that the letter of a subscripted variable refers to a block of storage locations, which is generally called an "array" or "matrix." An array may be one-dimensional like a motel or two-dimensional like a hotel. One- and two-dimensional arrays are sometimes called "lists" and "tables" respectively.

An array name must consist of just a single letter, and consequently we may have no more than 26 arrays within one program. A letter used as an array name may also be used as a simple variable within the same program. However, this practice can be confusing, and it is better to avoid it. The same array name may not be used for both a list and a table within a single program.

The value of a subscript must be a positive integer. The largest subscript value which is permitted in a program is called the "size" or "dimension" of the array. A table, referred to by a doubly subscripted variable, has two dimensions, the first dimension going with the first subscript and the second, with the second. When, for example, a 20 by 50 table is used, the first subscript may have values between 1 and 20 and the second, between 1 and 50. (Some versions of BASIC start counting at 0 rather than 1 for the smallest subscript value.)

Unless indicated otherwise, the computer automatically sets aside a block of memory locations for each array in a program large enough so that each subscript may take on values up to 10. This automatic feature may be overridden by using a DIM (dimension) statement. Thus the statement

50 DIM X(57),Q(25,30)

tells the computer to set aside 57 locations for the list X and 750 (25 times 30) locations for the table Q. One may also specify fewer locations than would automatically be assigned—for example,

60 DIM F(3)

It is good practice to dimension even small arrays in a DIM statement since this forces the programmer to think about how big each one really needs to be. If in doubt as to the required size, always overestimate. Too much room hurts nothing unless the resulting total program size exceeds the permissible limit of the computer, but reference within a program to an array location which does not exist—such as F(199) when F has been dimensioned by DIM F(3)—will cause the program to stop after the computer has sent an appropriate diagnostic.

There may be several DIM statements in a program, and they may occur anywhere within the program. Each DIM statement may contain as many array names as can be accommodated on the line, the array names being separated by commas.

When one member of an array is referenced within a program, the subscript may be a constant, a variable (simple or subscripted), or a formula. A nonintegral value will be truncated by the computer before it is used as a subscript. Therefore, if $N=3.7$ and $A(11)=3$, the symbols $X(3)$, $X(N)$, and $X(A(11))$ all refer to the same memory location—that is, the third member of the list X.

As an example of the use of loops and arrays, the following program reads 12 constants from the data list, puts them into the array list T, and computes and prints the sum and the sum of the squares of *every other* constant.

```
10 DIM T(12)
20 LET S=0
30 LET Q=0
```
```
40 FØR K=1 TØ 12
50 READ T(K)
60 NEXT K
```
```
70 FØR J=1 TØ 12 STEP 2
80 LET S=S+T(J)
90 LET Q=Q+T(J)↑2
100 NEXT J
```
```
110 PRINT S,Q
120 DATA 5,3,9,2,27,34,16,8,13,11,25,7
130 END
```

Note that in each of the two loops the counter (K in the first loop and J in the second) is also used as a subscript for the array T.

Actually in the above problem it is not necessary to use an array. As a general rule, arrays should be used only when the data needs to be accessed nonsequentially or altered during the execution of the program. In programs where the data can be processed sequentially, there is seldom any need to complicate matters by using arrays. The above program could have been written more simply as follows:

```
10 LET S=0
20 LET Q=0
```
```
30 FØR K=1 TØ 6
40 READ X,Y
50 LET S=S+X
60 LET Q=Q+X↑2
70 NEXT K
```
```
80 PRINT S,Q
90 DATA 5,3,9,2,27,34,16,8,13,11,23,7
100 END
```

For a program in which an array must be used, consider the program on the next page whose purpose is to take a list of constants and sort them so they occur in order of increasing size. The general problem of sorting is often encountered, and several algorithms are available for its solution. You might try to think up a different way from that shown. As a start, do the sorting manually and then write a program to reproduce your procedure. The algorithm for the program shown involves scanning the list from left to right, comparing every value with its right-hand neighbor and, if necessary, interchanging them so as to move the larger number toward the right of the list.

For example, let the initial list contain the four constants 7,5,9,3 (in the order given). First compare 7 and 5. As 7 is larger than 5, interchange them. The list now appears: 5,7,9,3. Next compare 7 and 9. 7 is not larger than 9; so move on and compare 9 and 3. 9 is larger than 3; so interchange them. At this point the largest number, 9, has been moved to the right side of the list (check that it would have done so regardless of where it was in the initial list). Note that with four numbers in the list, three comparisons were necessary on this first set of comparisons (the first "pass"). Now repeat the whole procedure with the new list but temporarily delete the 9. This second pass will require only two comparisons, and at its conclusion the entire list will be: 5,3,7,9. One more pass with just the one comparison between the first two elements gives the final list: 3,5,7,9.

In general if the list contains N values, N-1 passes will be required. The first pass will require N-1 comparisons, and this number is decreased by one for each succeeding pass.

The program on the next page says in BASIC what has just been said in English and should be thoroughly studied and analyzed. Note that by changing lines 10 (the length of the list of numbers), 20 (the data itself), and 30 (the dimension of the array), the same program will sort a list of any size.

```
10 LET N=4
20 DATA 7,5,9,3
30 DIM A(4)
40 FØR K=1 TØ N
50 READ A(K)
60 NEXT K
70 FØR M=1 TØ N−1
80 FØR J=1 TØ N−M
90 IF A(J+1)>A(J) THEN 130
100 LET X=A(J)
110 LET A(J)=A(J+1)
120 LET A(J+1)=X
130 NEXT J
140 NEXT M
150 FØR L=1 TØ N
160 PRINT A(L),
170 NEXT L
180 END
```

In this program the K-loop (lines 40 to 60) reads the data into the list array A. Each repetition of the M-loop (lines 70 to 140) corresponds to one pass, as described earlier. The J-loop (lines 80 to 130) is nested within the M-loop, and each repetition of it compares two adjacent elements in the current list. Note that the final value of the J-loop is decreased by one each time M takes on its next value. Lines 100 to 120 within the J-loop interchange two adjacent elements if necessary. (Note the use of the "temporary" variable X for making this switch.) Finally the L-loop (lines 150 to 170) produces a printout of the sorted list, five values on each line.

5.5 Questions

1 Consider the following program:

```
100 LET N=1
110 FØR J=1 TØ 3
```

```
120 LET N=N*J
130 PRINT N,
140 NEXT J
150 END
```

a Debug the program.

b What will the printout be?

c What will the printout be if we replace line 110 by

   110 FØR J=1 TØ 3 STEP 2

d What will happen if we replace line 110 by

   110 FØR J=3 TØ 1

e What will the printout be if we replace line 110 by

   110 FØR J=3 TØ 1 STEP −1

f What will happen if we add to the original program the line

   125 IF N>=2 THEN 140

2 Consider the following program:

```
100 DIM C(25)
110 DATA 5,21,10,13,7,6
120 READ N
130 FØR K=1 TØ N
140 READ C(K)
150 NEXT K
160 END
```

You will note that the program simply reads some data into the list array C.

a Will the program run if line 100 is deleted entirely?

    b What value will be stored in C(3) before the loop is started?

    c What value will be stored in C(3) after the loop is done?

3 Instead of specifying how many values are in a list of data, you can simply let the computer decide when the list is finished by providing a "marker" at the end of the data. The marker will be some constant whose value is an "impossible" one for the particular data being considered. The marker for a data list containing the heights of all of the students in a school could be some negative number such as -1, and a marker for the bank balances of an individual over several months could probably be 1.E20. The following program illustrates the use of such a device (the program accomplishes the same thing as the one in the previous question).

```
100 DIM C(25)
110 LET K=0
120 READ X
130 IF X=999999 THEN 180
140 LET K=K+1
150 LET C(K)=X
160 GØ TØ 120
170 DATA 21,10,13,7,6,999999
180 END
```

    a What is the marker?

    b What will be the value of K when line 180 is reached?

    c What would happen if the marker 999999 were removed from the data list?

4 The following program shows how to read data

into a table array. A similar set of statements could be used to print the values in a table.

```
100 DIM S(3,2)
110 DATA 12,17,3,19,7,21
120 FØR M=1 TØ 3
130 FØR J=1 TØ 2
140 READ S(M,J)
150 NEXT J
160 NEXT M
170 END
```

a Could line 100 be deleted without affecting the program?

b What constant will be stored in S(2,1) when the two loops are completed?

c What will be the value of M when the constant 7 in the data list is read?

d What would happen if lines 150 and 160 were interchanged?

e If the statements in lines 120 and 130 were interchanged as well as those in lines 150 and 160, the loops would still be nested; in what location would the constant 7 in the data list now be stored after the execution of two loops?

5.6 Answers

1 a There are no errors.

b 1   2   6

Note that the value of N after the loop has been completed is 3! (3 factorial, which is 1*2*3=6). By replacing the final value of the loop by, say, 100 rather than 3, the loop would calculate 100!

    c 1   3

    d In most versions of BASIC the loop will not be executed at all, and there will be no printout although the program will run. In some versions, however, the loop will be executed once, even though the counter's initial value is greater than the final value.

    e 3   6   6

    f Because N takes on the value 2 in line 120 during the second execution of the loop and 6 during the third, there will be only one number printed, the constant 1 during the first execution of the loop.

2 *a* Yes, because the maximum subscript value called for on the program is 5, which is less than the automatically provided value of 10. To save space in the computer's memory, we could write

    100 DIM C(5)

    b Either zero or garbage depending upon the particular BASIC.

    c 13. The 5 goes into N, the 21 into C(1), etc.

3 *a* The constant 999999, which presumably is not a possible value for the data to be processed.

    b 5, because K has been incremented by one each time an element of the data list, except the marker, was read.

    c At the sixth repetition of the READ statement in line 120, the program would stop with an "ØUT ØF DATA" message.

4 *a* Yes, because the automatic feature will provide the necessary subscript ranges for this program.

b 3.

c 3. The 7 will be stored in S(3,1).

d The program would not run as the two loops would then be overlapping rather than nested.

e S(2,2). The moral of this question is that one must be careful when handling tables, because it is very easy to get the subscripts confused.

5.7 Exercises

1 Write and run a program to do the following:

a Read the following six numbers into the list array G:

2,3,5,7,11,13

b Transfer the values in the list G to another list H so they appear in H in reverse order—that is H(1)=13, etc.

c Print both lists so they appear side by side on the paper.
Your printout should look like this:

2	13
3	11
5	7
7	5
11	3
13	2

For each of the three operations use a FØR-TØ loop rather than a sequence of six replacement, READ, or PRINT statements.

2 Write and run a program to do the following problem. Use FØR-TØ loops for each part.

a Read the data from the 2 by 3 table shown below into the 2 by 3 array X. X(1,1) should contain 4, X(1,2) should contain 7, etc. The usual mathematical convention is that the first subscript refers to the row number of a table and the second subscript to the column number.

```
4  7  8
2  3  1
```

b Print the table as it appears above.

c Print the table in transposed position—that is, as a 3 by 2 table; the resulting table should appear as shown below.

```
4    2
7    3
8    1
```

3 Write a program to compute and print the mean, standard deviation, median and mode(s) of a set of class scores. (See project one, Appendix C).

library functions and the DEF statement

6.1 Library Functions

There are certain mathematical functions which must be used in many problems but are quite difficult to program. For example, finding the value of one of the trigonometric functions is a simple-sounding task but is actually a rather arduous one to perform on a digital computer, and the use of the calculus is required to find an appropriate algorithm. Several of the common functions have been preprogrammed in BASIC and are available for use. The general form of these functions, called "library functions," is a 3-letter name followed by the number to be operated upon (the function argument) enclosed in parentheses. The following library functions are available in all versions of BASIC (your BASIC may have additional ones); if any of them are unfamiliar to you, ignore them. The variable X represents the function argument.

SIN(X): to find the sine of X, X in radians

CØS(X): to find the cosine of X, X in radians

TAN(X): to find the tangent of X, X in radians

ATN(X): to find the arctangent (principal value in radians) of X

EXP(X): to find the value of e raised to the X power where e is the base of natural logarithms; rounded to eight significant digits, $e = 2.7182818$

LØG(X): to find the natural logarithm of X

SQR(X): to find the square root of X

ABS(X): to find the absolute value of X

SGN(X): gives -1, 0, or 1 when X is negative, zero, or positive respectively

INT(X): the greatest integer function (see section 6.3)

RND(X): random number generator (see section 6.4)

TAB(X): to print in Specific Column (see section 7.3)

The argument of a library function may be a constant, a variable, or a formula. The function itself may be looked upon as a formula and used anywhere a formula is valid. Hence the following statement is legal (although not particularly meaningful):

    40 LET G=SQR(SIN(X+16)*ATN(LØG(47−K/X)))

Note that the argument of any of the trigonometric library functions must be in radians. To convert from degrees to radians, multiply degrees by 0.0174533 or divide degrees by 57.2957795. Thus to place the sine of 35° into location W, we can write

    60 LET W=SIN(35*.0174533)

You will probably have observed that the SQR function is not really needed, as the same operation is performed by raising the argument to the one-half power—

that is, $X\uparrow(1/2)$ or $X\uparrow.5$. Nevertheless, SQR is a standard part of the library and is preferred to the power form, since it usually executes faster.

The time difference in the two methods is trivial if you have only a few such computations to make but will probably become apparent if the number goes into the thousands.

The logarithm to the base 10 of X can be found by dividing the natural logarithm of X by the natural logarithm of 10. Thus

50 LET T=LØG(4)/LØG(10)

will place the common logarithm of 4 into location T.

The SGN function will occasionally save a little programming effort. For example,

40 ØN SGN(T)+2 GØ TØ 70,100,35

will cause the program to branch to line 70, 100, or 35, depending on whether the value of T is negative, zero, or positive respectively. The same action could be produced by using two IF-THEN statements and a GØ TØ, but the use of the SGN function is much easier.

The ABS function gives the magnitude of the argument. Thus, ABS(5.2)=5.2, ABS(0)=0, and ABS(−5.2)= 5.2.

6.2 The DEF Statement

It may happen that some complicated formula is needed in several places within one program. To save some programming effort, functions of your own may be defined by using the DEF statement. For example, assume you need to calculate the area of a circle (given the radius) in a number of places in a program and for different values of the radius. Before reaching the first such calculation, write the statement

    20 DEF FNA(X)=3.14159265*X↑2

Then if the area of a circle of radius 5.3 is desired, write

    70 LET C=FNA(5.3)

The computer would replace X in the definition of the function FNA by 5.3, do the indicated calculation, and place the result in C.

The name of a function defined by a DEF statement must contain three letters, the first two being FN and the third being an arbitrary letter (hence a maximum of 26 functions may be defined in one program). In the DEF statement the argument of the function (X in the above example) is a "dummy" variable and is used only to indicate what calculations are to be performed; any single letter may be used.

6.3 The INT Function

The INT function is the "greatest integer" function, which you may have encountered at one time or another. It is used by itself to round or truncate constants for printing or other purposes and is extremely useful in conjunction with the RND function, to be discussed in the next section.

The value of INT(X) is the greatest integer which is less than or equal to X. If we think of X being located on a number scale going from negative infinity at the left to positive infinity at the right, then INT(X) is equal to X itself if X is an integer and otherwise is equal to the first integer to the left of X. Thus INT(5)=5, INT(7.8)=7, INT(0.9)=0, INT(−5)=−5, and (look carefully) INT(−3.2)=−4.

To round a constant to the nearest integer, for example, the statement

    10 LET Y=INT(X+.5)

may be used. In this statement if $X=4.2$, then $X+.5=4.7$, and $INT(X+.5)=4$; if $X=3.7$, $X+.5=4.2$, and $INT(X+.5)=4$. The algorithm also produces the correct result if X is negative, as can be readily verified.

Rounding a constant to the nearest tenth is a bit more difficult but can be done by

    10 LET Y=INT(10*X+.5)/10

If $X=4.73$, $10*X+.5=47.3+.5=47.8$, INT $(10*X+.5)=47$; so INT $(10*X+.5)/10=4.7$.

6.4 The RND Function

Some of the most interesting applications of digital computers occur in simulating certain situations where randomness in one form or another is encountered. Such situations range anywhere from tossing a coin to fighting wars. A complete study of the problems involved in setting up a simulation is well beyond the scope of this book, but the key tool, the RND function, is not.

The statements

    30 RANDOMIZE*
    40 LET H=RND(X)

selects "at random" a number between 0 (inclusive) and 1 (exclusive) and places it in location H. In effect we may think of the computer having a round card with a spinner mounted at the center and a uniform, continuous scale from 0 to 1 going around the edge of the card. The 0 and the

*Required by some computer systems at the beginning of a program.

1 are located at the same physical point which is called "zero." When a RND function is encountered in a program, the computer spins the spinner and records the number at which the spinner points when it stops. As the spinner is just as likely to stop one place as another, the resulting number is a "random" one (with a "uniform" distribution).

Actually a random number is generated by a relatively complicated mathematical procedure, but we need not be concerned here with the exact algorithm. We should mention that the numbers are in reality not genuinely random numbers and in fact are more properly spoken of as being "pseudorandom." However, a long sequence of these generated numbers has many of the properties of a truly random sequence, and normally no difficulty arises by using the numbers produced by the computer.

You may be questioning what role the argument X plays in this function. The answer is none, usually. There are considerable differences in various versions of BASIC as to this argument; some, in fact, delete it entirely, using simply

```
10 LET H=RND
```

With most versions of BASIC each execution of the same program containing RND functions will produce the same sequence of random numbers. This is a convenient feature, as it facilitates debugging a program, but occasionally one wishes to run a program several times with different sequences. All BASIC versions have some way of doing this: some use a statement such as RANDØMIZE at the beginning of the program, and some use special constants for the argument of the RND function. Again, the manufacturer's manual, possibly aided by experience, should clear up the matter. If local knowledge is nonexistent, we suggest you experiment with various possibilities. It is sometimes faster and simpler to try things on the computer than to obtain information from a book, manual, or person, and it is usually more educational as well as more fun.

Most experiments that one might wish to simulate require random numbers other than those uniformly distributed on the interval from 0 to 1, as produced by the unmodified RND function. We will give two examples to show how such problems can be handled but will not attempt to cover the topic in any great detail.

A coin-tossing experiment can be simulated by generating a random sequence of 0s and 1s, where a 1 will indicate a head and a 0 a tail, and where 0s and 1s each occur with probability .5. Consider the statement

50 LET C=INT(RND(X)+.5)

When this statement is executed, RND(X) will be some number between 0 and 1, and RND(X)+.5 a number between .5 and 1.5. Consequently the final result of the formula will be either 0 or 1, each with probability .5. The coin could be biased in favor of heads by adding .6 rather than .5 to RND(X); heads would then occur with probability .6 and tails .4.

To simulate tossing a die where the outcomes are the integers 1 through 6 and are equally likely, we can use

50 LET D=INT(6*RND(X))+1

You should verify that this statement will give the desired results.

6.5 Questions

1 What value will be assigned to Y by each of the following statements?

> *a* LET Y=SGN(−4.2)
>
> *b* LET Y=INT(−4.2)
>
> *c* LET Y=ABS(−4.2)
>
> *d* LET Y=INT(SGN(−4.2))

2 Consider the following program:

```
10 DEF FNX(A)=A↑2−3*A+2
20 LET M=4
30 LET B1=FNX(M)
40 LET B2=FNX(M/2+1)
50 PRINT B1,B2
60 END
```

a What value will be assigned to B1 by line 30?

b What value will be assigned to B2 by line 40?

3 If N = −6, to which line will a program be directed by the statement

```
40 ØN SGN(N)+2 GØ TØ 50,10,90
```

4 Write a replacement statement that will store in C the value of the constant in T rounded to the nearest one-hundredth.

5 Write a statement which will assign to D a random integer between 1 and 100 inclusive.

6 Consider the following program which simulates tossing a coin 100 times. A head is represented by 1 and a tail by 2. The number of occurrences of heads and tails is stored in X(1) and X(2) respectively.

```
10 DIM X(2)
20 LET X(1)=0
30 LET X(2)=0
40 FØR K=1 TØ 100
50 LET N=INT(RND(X)+1.5)
60 LET X(N)=X(N)+1
70 NEXT K
80 PRINT X(1),X(2)
90 END
```

  a What are the possible values of the constant assigned to N in line 50?

  b What is the relationship between the values of K, X(1), and X(2) each time line 70 is reached?

  c Add statements to the program so that it will simulate ten people each tossing a coin 100 times.

 7 What is the probability a 1 will be assigned to V by the statement

  60 LET V=INT(RND(X)+.3)

6.6 Answers

  1 a −1.

   b −5.

   c 4.2.

   d −1.

  2 a 6.

   b 2, because M/2+1=3.

  3 To line 50.

  4 LET C=INT(100*T+.5)/100

  5 LET D=INT(100*RND(X))+1 or
   LET D=INT(100*RND(X)+1)

  6 a Either 1 or 2; each value is equally likely.

   b As X(1) holds the number of heads, X(2) the number of tails, and K the number of tosses, K=X(1)+X(2).

c This is most easily done by nesting the given program inside another loop, which will be executed 10 times. Thus

```
15 FØR J=1 TØ 10
85 NEXT J
```

Note that the new loop must start before line 20 in order to initialize the counters X(1) and X(2) to zero before each person begins.

7 .3.

6.7 Exercises

1 Write and run a program which will simulate tossing a regular six-sided die 60 times. Count and print the number of times each side comes up. It will be convenient to use a list array of dimension 6 to keep track of the counting.

2 Write a program which will simulate the tossing of a coin 100 times. Count and print the number of times heads appeared, tails appeared as well as a per cent comparison of each.

input, printing, and string data

7.1 The INPUT Statement

We have previously discussed two ways in which data can be put into the computer: the replacement (LET) statement and the READ-DATA statement pair. A third method uses the INPUT statement, as in the program

```
20 INPUT X,Y
30 PRINT X,Y
40 END
```

When the computer reaches line 20 during the execution of the program, it types a question mark; the user replies with the constants which he/she wishes to have assigned to the variables X and Y. The two constants are typed on the same line, separated by a comma; then the RETURN key is struck. The computer stores the constants in the desired locations and proceeds with the program.

The variable list following the word INPUT may contain as many variables as desired, and they may be of any type: simple, subscripted, or—to be discussed later— string.

When the computer types the question mark, the user must respond with as many constants as there are variables in the INPUT list. If this is not done, another question mark will be sent by the computer.

It is desirable in many programs to put a PRINT statement just before each INPUT statement; this will print the symbols for the variables whose values are being requested. Thus we might add to the above program the statement

```
10 PRINT "X,Y"
```

The computer would then type

```
X,Y
?
```

Putting a semicolon at the end of the PRINT statement will cause the question mark to be placed immediately after the Y rather than on a new line. Thus

```
10 PRINT "X,Y";
```

in our program will produce

```
X,Y?
```

A more informative message, such as WHAT ARE THE VALUES ØF X AND Y, could also be used.

The INPUT statement opens up the possibility of some rather interesting conversation interaction between the computer and the user during the execution of a program and is important in tutorial programs in which the computer plays the role of a teacher. It is also used to supply a small amount of data to "public library" programs; these are available on most computers to handle routine problems which the user would prefer not to program himself/herself or problems whose complexity or sophistication are beyond the programming capabilities of the user.

It is faster and more economical to enter data by the

READ and DATA statements rather than by the INPUT statement, but you should become acquainted with the latter since it is very handy in some situations.

7.2 Advanced Printing

Up to this point our print format has been limited to no more than five constants on one line. In this section we shall consider one way of increasing the versatility of the print format. In programs where there is a relatively small amount of output and/or one is not too concerned with how the printout looks, the standard format is usually adequate; occasionally one needs—or wants—to be a bit more sophisticated. We might mention that one of the joys of BASIC is its ability to accept input data and produce output data with very little effort on the part of the programmer. Most other programming languages require a great deal of attention to the format of both input and output, and this is generally a formidable obstacle for the beginning student.

More than five constants may be printed on a line by replacing the commas in the PRINT statement list by semicolons. This tells the computer to reduce the width of a print field from the standard number of spaces (usually 15) to some smaller value. The actual number of spaces will depend upon how many characters are needed to represent the constant being printed as well as the particular BASIC being used. One fairly common rule is that the print field will be 6 spaces for 1- to 3-digit numbers, 9 spaces for 4- to 6-digit numbers, 12 spaces for 7- to 9-digit numbers, and 15 for 10 or more digits. The BASIC manual for your particular system should give the details, but some experimentation will probably be simpler. It should be clear that using the semicolon option can save considerable time if there are many short constants to be printed. Unfortunately it is possible to get into trouble at the end of a print line and have several digits of one number printed on top of each other; therefore be cautious if the entire line is to be filled.

Using the semicolon with messages produces a print field width equal to the length of the message itself, and this can greatly improve the appearance of a printout. For example, if the variable X has been assigned the value of 25, the statement

     60 PRINT "X = ",X

produces

     X =   25

whereas

     60 PRINT "X = ";X

produces

     X = 25

Some versions of BASIC give the same result with messages if the separator—the semicolon or comma—between the message and the following expression is simply deleted.

7.3   The PRINT TAB(X) Statement

The TAB(X) statement is a convenient way to specify where printing is to begin. TAB(X) can be used to print information in uniform columns or to plot results or make fancy computer pictures.

     100 PRINT TAB(20); "GARY BITTER"

This statement will print GARY BITTER starting in column 20. The TAB starts counting from column one,* left to right.

---

*Some systems the print will begin in column 19 as they start counting in Column 0.

For example:

```
10 PRINT TAB(5); "BITTER"
20 PRINT TAB(10); "BITTER"
30 PRINT TAB(15); "BITTER"
40 PRINT TAB(20); "BITTER"
50 PRINT TAB(25); "BITTER"
60 END
```

will give the printout:

```
BITTER
      BITTER
            BITTER
                  BITTER
                        BITTER
```

The PRINT TAB can also carry out computations for the variable X.

```
10 LET C=55
20 LET D=40
30 PRINT TAB(C−5); D; TAB(C+5); D
40 END
```

This will print 40 beginning in column 50 and column 60. The TAB statement can be used for spacing, making tabular print-out or graphing.

Most versions of BASIC now have additional features for increasing the flexibility of the printout format. Because of the wide variety of methods and the fact that the time and energy spent on programming a nonstandard format are seldom well spent by the beginning student, we will not carry the discussion further. When you feel ready to become concerned about the problem, a perusal of the appropriate BASIC manual for your computer should set you on the right path.

7.4 String Data and Variables

Some versions of BASIC permit reading, manipulating, and printing nonnumeric data. If your BASIC does not, skip this section.

For this purpose we use what are known as "string variables." A string variable refers in the same manner as simple and subscripted variables to a location in the memory of the computer, with the difference that the location is set up to hold symbolic characters rather than numbers. The term "character" includes all the symbols normally used in BASIC—letters, numerals, punctuation, and operation and relation symbols—as well as several others which appear on the terminal keyboard. One variable (memory location) holds up to fifteen or more characters. The collection of characters in one variable is called a "word" or a "string."

A string variable is identified by one letter followed by a dollar sign—for example, A$. Thus we may use no more than 26 simple string variables in a program. However we may also set up a list array for character (string) data and use a singly subscripted string variable to identify the locations. The size of such a list is declared in a DIM statement if the standard size of 10 is not sufficient. You may *not* use a doubly subscripted string variable.

The desired characters may be assigned to a string variable by a READ statement, a replacement (LET) statement, or an INPUT statement.

When using a READ statement, the words in the DATA statement list are separated by commas. If a word starts with a nonalphabetic character or contains a comma or leading or trailing blanks (a blank is a legal character), the entire word must be enclosed in quotation marks. The statements

```
50 READ A$,B$(1),B$(2)
60 DATA JØE WAS BØRN ØN, " JAN.1,","1937"
```

will place the 15-character word

>   JØE WAS BØRN ØN

into A$, the 7-character word (including one leading blank)

>   JAN. 1,

into B$(1), and the 4-character word

>   1937

into B$(2). If a word in the DATA list does not take up all the room in a memory location, the location will be filled the rest of the way to the right with blank characters.

The LET statement may be used by putting the word to be stored on the right side of the equals sign and enclosing the word with a pair of quotation marks—for example,

>   60 LET X$="BE PREPARED"

String data is written for entry via an INPUT statement, just as it is for a DATA statement.

Numerical and string variables may be mixed in both INPUT and READ statements; the corresponding data must of course be mixed similarly. For example, the following two statements would execute satisfactorily:

>   20 READ A$,B,C$,
>   30 DATA SIX,6,"6"

Although it is beyond the scope of this book to consider the actual methods of coding, we stress the fact that different representations of the number 6 are stored in B and C$. The former is such a form as can be used in arithmetic operations while the latter is not. Hence the expression $2*B$ is quite legal, but $2*C\$$ is illegal and would result in a diagnostic.

The words stored in string variables may be printed by using a PRINT statement in the normal way. For example, if X$ has been assigned the word "BE PREPARED", the statement

    70 PRINT X$

will produce the printout

    BE PREPARED

    Note that a message included in a PRINT statement is not a string constant; so the restriction to 15 characters does not apply to messages.

    Although string data may not be operated upon in the same way as numerical data—in arithmetic expressions, for example—a comparison may be made between the "values" of two string variables or of one string variable and one string constant by using an IF-THEN statement. Any of the six relations may be used. In general one word is "less than" another in exactly the same way that one word comes before another in a dictionary. Thus BALL is "less than" BARN, but MØØN is "greater than" MØØ. The ordering of the nonalphabetic symbols varies among different versions of BASIC, and an appropriate manual should be consulted if necessary.

    It might be pointed out that the program in Chapter 5 for ordering a list of numbers can be changed to one for alphabetizing a list of words by changing the array A and the simple variable X to a string array and a string variable respectively. For example, replace A by A$ and X by X$. (See exercise 4).

    When a string constant is used in an IF-THEN statement, it must be enclosed in quotation marks:

    80 IF X$ = "CØØL IT" THEN 150

7.5 Questions

1 Consider the following program:

```
100 LET S=0
110 INPUT M
120 FØR J=1 TØ 3
130 LET S=S+M
140 NEXT J
150 PRINT S
160 END
```

a How many times will the computer stop and ask for a number to be typed in?

b If the number 5 is typed in when line 110 is executed, what number will be printed at line 150?

c If the line number of the INPUT statement is changed from 110 to 125, how many numbers will have to be typed in during the execution of the program?

d If the change suggested in c is made and the values 5, 6, and 7 are typed in, what number will be printed?

2 Consider the following program:

```
10 DATA 1,2,3
20 READ A,B,C
30 PRINT A,B,C
40 END
```

a What will the printout be?

b If line 30 is replaced by 30 PRINT A;B;C, what will the printout be?

c If line 30 is replaced by 30 PRINT A;B,C, what will the printout be?

3 Identify each of the following variables as to type and legality: X, $X, X(1), X$, X1(1), X1$, X(1,1), X$(1), X1(1,1), X$(1,1).

4 Must each of the strings given below be enclosed in quotation marks when written in a data list?

  a 23 SKIDØØ

  b A, B, AND C

  c U.S.A.

5 Debug each of the following statements:

  a 90 LET P$=I LIKE IKE

  b 90 LET P="I LIKE IKE"

  c 90 IF G$<=LØVE THEN 900

  d 90 IF G$><"LOVE" THEN 900

  e 90 IF G$<>"LOVE", THEN 900

7.6 Answers

  1 a 1.

    b 15. The loop is executed three times, and each time 5, the value of M, is added to S.

    c 3.

    d 18.

  2 a 1   2   3

    b 1   2   3

    that is, the printing will be "packed."

    c 1   2   3

  3 X is a legal simple variable. $X is illegal. X(1) is a legal singly subscripted variable. X$ is a legal

string variable. X1(1) is illegal. X1$ is illegal. X(1,1) is a legal doubly subscripted variable. X$(1) is a legal singly subscripted string variable. X1(1,1) is illegal. X$(1,1) is illegal.

4 *a* Yes, because it starts with a numerical character.

b Yes, because it contains commas.

c No, but quotation marks may be used.

5 *a* The string on the right side of the equals sign must be enclosed in quotation marks.

b The variable is of the wrong type; it must be a string variable.

c The string LØVE must be enclosed in quotation marks.

d The relation symbol is illegal; presumably it should be $<>$.

e No comma after "LØVE".

7.7 Exercises

1 Write and run a program which during execution will request the value of a number and then compute and print, along with an appropriate message, the number and its square root. The complete printout during execution should appear as follows, where the underlined number is typed in by the user during execution:

WHAT IS THE NUMBER? <u>25</u>
THE SQUARE RØØT ØF 25 IS 5

2 (Do only if your BASIC permits string data manipulation.) Write and run a program which will do the following:

a The computer types "DØES $2+2=4$" followed by a question mark which is generated by an INPUT statement.

b If the user replies "YES", the computer types "YØU ARE WØNDERFUL", and the program stops.

c If the user replies "NØ", the computer types "TRY AGAIN", a question mark, and waits for another response.

d If the user replies with something other than "YES" or "NØ", the computer types "HUH", a question mark, and waits for a response.

e If a "YES" is not obtained in two responses, the computer types "NINCØMPØØP", and the program stops.

Drawing a careful flowchart for this problem before attempting to write the program will be time well spent. It is not a long program but needs to be thought out.

3 Write a program to test a person in the basic multiplication facts. Generate the facts randomly and have the person give answers via the terminal. Check each answer and if wrong give a second chance. Print wrong when person gives incorrect answer. After twenty-five problems print percent correct.

4 Write and run a program to alphabetize a list of names. Hint: See program page 89.

the end and
the beginning

8.1 Introduction

In this final chapter we will mention a few capabilities
which most versions of BASIC share but which have not
been covered so far; we will rely upon your ability to read
the necessary manuals as the need for them arises.

8.2 Library Programs

In many time-sharing systems there are a large number of
complete programs stored within the computer which are
available to any user. These programs constitute the "public
library." A catalog of library programs should be available
at your terminal, and it is worth a few minutes of your time
to scan the list of what is there, since a user can save
considerable time and effort when faced with a more or
less standard problem whose solution has already been
programmed and is stored in the library. The description
of each program in the catalog includes the instructions for
entering data. Many of these programs are written in a
language other than BASIC (FORTRAN and ALGOL are
the most frequently used alternatives), but this is normally

of no consequence to the user. Some care should be exercised when using library programs, because they may not do exactly what the user thinks they do. It is generally a good practice to run one or two simple test cases for which the answers are known to make sure the operation of a program is clearly understood.

8.3 The GØSUB and RETURN Statements

The two statements GØSUB and RETURN permit certain portions of a program to be used repeatedly but in a manner quite different from that of a loop. Their use can be avoided in most programs, and some programmers prefer to do without them. When their use is appropriate, they can save considerable programming effort and should eventually become part of the serious student's programming equipment.

8.4 Editing Commands

A large number of system commands are available for the purpose of manipulating programs within a computer. We have listed and explained several in Appendix E. These editing commands can delete or retain selected parts of a program, provide a completely new set of line numbers (a great convenience if one needs to put another statement between lines 50 and 51, for example), merge two or more programs into one, or perform several other rather sophisticated operations on a program itself. They are fully described in the terminal manuals provided by the computer manufacturer or service bureau, and an acquaintance with them is well worthwhile.

8.5 MAT Statements

If you have been exposed to matrix algebra in your mathematical education, you are aware of the power and convenience the use of matrices brings to many problems. Most versions of BASIC provide a number of statements, the MAT statements, which perform matrix manipulations; their use is highly recommended when doing what are essentially matrix operations. For example, you may add or multiply two matrices or find the transpose or inverse of a matrix by using a single BASIC statement. The same operations can of course be programmed using only the statements presented in this book but usually at the cost of considerable effort.

If you are not acquainted with matrix algebra but intend to do many problems which involve handling large blocks or arrays of data, time spent in learning some of the elementary theory of the subject will be well spent.

8.6   Data Files

It is sometimes desirable to be able to save the results of one program for use in another one at a later time. This can be done by using the paper tape punch and reader on the terminal; but if a large amount of data is involved, it is an inconvenient and time-consuming procedure. Most versions of BASIC offer the much simpler alternative of using "data files," which are placed on the slow memory of a computer and are available for either input or output of data during the execution of a BASIC program. To use such a file, it is necessary to learn a few new BASIC statements. These statements as well as the specific file capabilities differ considerably between the many BASIC versions, and the specialized BASIC manuals should be consulted for details.

8.7   FORTRAN

Although this is a book about BASIC, a word concerning FORTRAN is not out of place. FORTRAN is the most widely used batch-processing programming language today; and if you continue to be involved with computers, you are certain to encounter it. Fortunately there is a great similarity between BASIC and FORTRAN, and students should have little trouble learning the latter if they are reasonably adept at the former. FORTRAN was developed in the late 1950s; although it has been used primarily with batch-processing computer systems, it is available on many time-sharing systems. If the facilities are available, it would be desirable to write a few programs in this older but usually more powerful language. The principal difficulty, as suggested in Chapter 7, will be reading data into a program and printing the results. A good starting point would be to translate a BASIC program into FORTRAN, because it can be done almost on a statement-by-statement basis.

8.8 Some Final Remarks

Locate a copy of the BASIC manual for your particular system and, as time permits, go through it in some detail. For the most part we have tried in this book to present material which is applicable to all versions of BASIC; consequently there are some features of each particular version which we have not covered.

We have mentioned from time to time the desirability of experimenting with the computer in order to settle a subtle point about its behavior. We suggest you take every opportunity to "play" a bit with the computer in order to learn more about its capabilities. If you look upon a computer as a superintelligent master, that is what it will be; but if it is viewed as a reasonably bright and very stubborn slave (with absolutely no feelings to be hurt), you can extract a great deal of help from it and greatly extend your own problem-solving capabilities.

APPENDIX A
using the ASR 33
Teletype Terminal

A.1 Introduction

This appendix will acquaint you with a typical remote terminal used in a time-sharing computer system and with some of the mechanics and vocabulary needed to converse with the computer.

The use of the word "typical" is regrettable but necessary. We noted in Chapter 1 the existence of many different dialects of BASIC, and we must here note the existence of several different kinds of terminals and sets of "system commands," the vocabulary used when communicating with the computer. We will not attempt to include a description of every possible terminal and will confine our remarks to one particular type, the ASR 33 Teletype, Figure 1, which is in widespread use and is more likely than not to be the one you will be using. If not, a perusal of the appropriate terminal manual for your system after you have read this chapter should set you straight as to how to proceed.

FIGURE 1 Model 33 Teletype Unit. (By permission of Teletype Corporation.)

The comments on the ASR 33 Teletype will usually apply in principle, although possibly not in detail, to other terminal types.

The keyboard, paper tape controls, and control unit are diagrammed in Figure 2. Comparing this with Figure 1 (or, even better, with an actual machine), you will see the paper tape controls at the left of the keyboard and the control unit at the right.

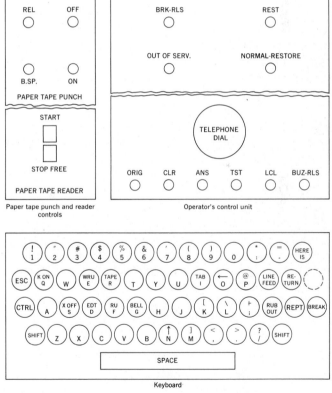

Paper tape punch and reader controls

Operator's control unit

Keyboard

FIGURE 2   **Model 33 Teletypewriter Keyboard and Controls**

Most of the keys on the keyboard have two symbols on them. When the key is struck, the lower symbol is printed unless one of the two SHIFT keys is depressed; in the latter case the upper symbol is printed. When the symbol is actually a short word, such as RUBOUT, X-ON, or WRU, nothing is printed but some action is taken. All letters are printed in uppercase. Note carefully that there are separate keys for the numeral "0" and the letter "O" and also for the numeral "1" and the letter "L." The members of each of these two pairs are not normally distinguished on a regular typewriter, and for human communication the message context serves to distinguish one from the other. Computers do not read in context; therefore explicit symbols are needed. When printed on the Teletype the 1 and the L are clearly different because the L is uppercase. The usual convention for distinguishing between the numeral 0 and the letter O is to put a diagonal slash through the latter; thus the symbol 0 is the numeral and Ø is the letter.

Some of the remaining symbols may be used in certain BASICs and in certain system commands. The space bar does not produce a symbol in the usual sense, but it does produce an electrical signal when struck. From the computer's viewpoint the space is just as effective a symbol as any other.

None of the short words on the upper part of some of the keys are used in this book and with one or two exceptions are not used in any version of BASIC. They refer to certain operations which are performed when a Teletype is used in its original manner to send messages back and forth between people.

The remaining keys on the keyboard and an indication of their uses are as follows:

> ESC (sometimes labeled ALT MODE): to delete an entire line when sending a message to the computer

CTRL: sometimes used in conjunction with other keys to stop the execution of a program

SHIFT: to obtain the upper symbol on a key

HERE IS: not used

LINE FEED: rolls the paper in the Teletype up one line

RETURN: returns the printing head to the left side of the paper; this key is depressed at the end of every line or message typed by the user

RUBOUT: produces a "do nothing" signal; used with paper tape

REPT: when held down together with another key causes the action of the latter to be repeated; used mostly with RUBOUT

BREAK: stops the activities of the computer (in some systems); its use must be followed by pushing the BRK-RLS button on the control unit

The following parts of the control unit are used:

Telephone dial or buttons: to call the computer

BRK-RLS: to reset after striking the BREAK key

ORIG: to originate a call

CLR: to turn off (clear) the Teletype; this is the "panic" button and may be used to disconnect the computer either normally or in an emergency (an emergency occurs when you need to do something but don't quite know what)

LCL: to use the Teletype in local mode—that is, when not connected to the computer; operation in this mode is called "offline" as contrasted to "online" when conversation with the computer is taking place; the Teletype is used offline when preparing a paper tape

BUZ-RLS: to turn off the buzzer which sounds when
the paper in the Teletype is about to run out

The small knob in front of the control unit (not
shown in Figure 2) controls the volume of the loud-
speaker; it should be set so that the ringing when the
computer is called is audible.

A.2 Paper Tape

Most terminals receive and print information from the
computer at the rate of about 10 characters per second and
are capable of sending at the same rate if the user can type
that fast. To utilize this sending capacity, and therefore to
save terminal time, which in most installations costs money,
we may make use of the paper tape punch and reader which
are located at the left of the Teletype keyboard. The punch
is used to prepare a paper tape of the program while the
Teletype is in the offline mode. The prepared tape is then
placed in the reader which sends the program to the computer at maximum speed after the computer is called and
the online mode established. Paper tape may also be used
to store an infrequently used program instead of storing
it in the computer's slow memory. In fact, if a program is
valuable, a paper tape copy should always be kept even
if the program is stored in the computer, because the computer's memory may be accidentally erased.

To prepare a paper tape of a program proceed as
follows:

1 Push the LCL button on the Teletype.

2 Turn on the paper tape punch by depressing the
ON button located on the punch unit (see Figure
2).

3 Put a "leader" on the tape by simultaneously
depressing the REPEAT and RUBOUT keys until

about 2 inches of tape have been punched. The RUBOUT will punch holes all across the tape, and this code will be ignored by the computer. The REPEAT causes repetition of the RUBOUT. The purpose of the leader is to allow easy handling of the tape when it is inserted into the reader.

4 Now type the program as usual but with one exception: after you depress the RETURN key at the end of a line, also depress the LINE FEED key and the RUBOUT key (in that order). When receiving a program by tape, the computer does not respond with a LINE FEED when a RETURN is encountered as it does when the user is typing online; you must provide your own LINE FEED. The signal RUBOUT is to give the print head on the Teletype time to return to the left side of the paper. Therefore remember: RETURN, LINE FEED, and RUBOUT at the end of each line.

5 When the program has been typed, depress the RUBOUT and REPEAT keys in order to punch approximately 2 more inches of tape, known as the "trailer."

6 Tear off the tape by pulling straight up. This will tear the tape so you will know which end is which.

7 Turn the tape punch off by pushing the OFF button on the punch, and push the CLR button to turn off the Teletype.

A paper tape copy of our example program is shown in Figure 3. The ends of the tape are automatically torn to indicate which is the beginning and which is the end. Each row of eight large holes or blanks represents one character; the small hole which is present in every row is the sprocket hole for the tape reader and is not part of the character code. If you are interested in knowing the codes for the various characters, your computer director can sup-

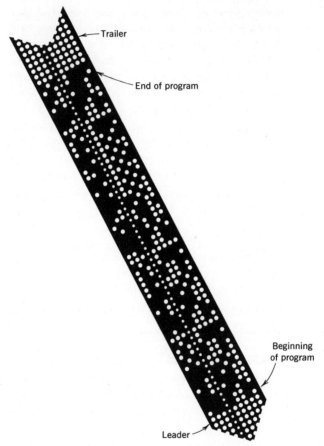

FIGURE 3 **Paper Tape of Sample Program**

ply you with the information; but it is normally of no consequence to the user. You might note the RUBOUT code (eight holes) which marks the end of each line of the program. One inch of tape holds 10 characters, so the tape will be read at the rate of about one inch per second.

To read a tape to the computer, proceed as follows:

1 Before you call up the computer, insert the prepared paper tape into the tape reader. Be sure it
is inserted in the correct way with the sprocket
wheel teeth in the sprocket holes. If in doubt, have
someone show you, for it is easier to do than to
describe. The tape reader switch should be in the
STOP (middle) position.

2 Call the computer, and when the computer has
responded with READY after you have given the
program name, type TAPE. (Do not try to use the
upper symbol on the R key; it won't work.)

3 When the computer again types READY, push the
tape reader switch to the START (upper) position.
The program will be sent to the computer and also
printed on the Teletype. A slight misalignment of
the tape in the reader may garble the program.
If this occurs (it will be obvious from the printout
on the Teletype), remove the tape, and try again.
A garble may cause the computer to turn the
Teletype off entirely, in which case you must start
all over.

4 When the tape reader stops at the end of the tape,
push the reader switch to the STOP position and
type the user command KEY which tells the computer that you are going to resume using the
keyboard.

5 When the computer types READY, proceed as
usual.

6 The tape may be easily removed from the reader
by pushing the reader switch to the FREE (bottom)
position and pulling the tape out.

Figure 4 shows the entire output of a run using
paper tape.

It is sometimes desirable to make a paper tape copy
of a program which is in the computer—for example, after

```
ASU35478


TIME-SHARING SERVICE


ØN AT    8:11    PX SYSF 2/2/78 TTY 17

ACCØUNT NUMBER--EDBITTER
PRØJECT ID----2ED691
SYSTEM--BASIC
NEW ØR ØLD--NEW
NEW FILE NAME--GARY
READY.

TAPE
READY.

10 LET X=25
20 LET Y=15
30 PRINT X,Y,X+Y,X-Y,X*Y
40 END
KEY
READY.

RUN
WAIT.

GARY     8:12    PX SYSF 2/2/78

25       15       40       10       375



USED    1.50 UNITS.
BYE

*** ØFF AT  8:12   ELAPSED TERMINAL TIME =   1 MIN.
```

FIGURE 4   **Sample Program Using Paper Tape**

a program has been debugged. To do this, get the program into the working file (use the ØLD command if it isn't already there) and give the command LISTNH. *Before* you push the RETURN key following the LISTNH, turn on the paper tape punch and punch a leader; then push RETURN. The program will be typed on the Teletype and also punched on the tape. When the listing is finished, punch a trailer on the tape and turn off the punch. Note that using LISTNH rather than LIST prevents a heading from being punched on the tape. Such a heading could lead to difficulties when the tape was read back to the computer because the computer would try to interpret the program name in the heading as a user command.

A tape may be listed offline by running it through the reader after first pushing the LCL button. A duplicate tape may be made by reading the original tape offline while the punch is turned on.

APPENDIX B

additional exercises

GEOMETRY

1 Write a program which will find the third side of a right triangle using the Pythagorean theorem.

2 Write a program which will determine the angle between two intersecting lines.

3 Write a program which will give the number of flat faces of a polyhedron using Euler's formula.

ALGEBRA

1 Write a program which will solve quadratic equations using the quadratic formula.

2 Write a program which will carry out synthetic division.

3 Write a program which will solve two equations in two unknowns.

NUMBER THEORY

1 Write a program which will print out Pascal's triangle for $n \leq 100$.

2 Write a program using the Sieve of Eratosthenes scheme for locating prime numbers. Print the first 100 prime numbers.

3 Write a program to print out all the pentagonal numbers between 1 and 3,000.

4 Write a program to generate the first fifty numbers of the Fibonacci sequence.

TRIGONOMETRY

1 Write a program which will find the three angles of a triangle given the three sides.

2 Write a program which will determine whether three given sides form a right triangle.

3 Write a program which will generate the values of tangent in radians.

PROBABILITY AND STATISTICS

1 Write a program which will find the mean and standard deviation of a given sample.

2 Write a program which will use a Monte Carlo method to approximate π.

3 Write a program simulating the roulette wheel.

4 Write a program to predict local population growth or decline based on previous census totals.

LINEAR ALGEBRA

1 Write a program which will find the inverse of a matrix.

2 Write a program to find the rank of a matrix.

3 Write a program to find the product of two matrices.

PSYCHOLOGY

1 Three groups of rats are run in a Skinner box (bar-pressing for food reinforcements) under three shock levels. Write a program that will determine whether there is a significant effect of shock level on response rate.

2 Write a program that will give you the correlation between college board scores and grade point averages for a group of students.

3 Write a computer assisted test with final score printout.

POLITICAL SCIENCE

1 Write a computer program which:
   a Reads the precinct number, the Democratic vote, and the Republican vote from five voting precincts
   b Computes both the Democratic percentage vote and the Republican percentage vote for each of the five precincts
   c Accumulates the vote totals for all five precincts
   d Computes the total Democratic percentage vote and the total Republican percentage vote for all five precincts
   e Rounds all the percentages to one decimal place
   f Prints the percentage results for both the five individual precincts and the five precincts totaled together

2 Using an INPUT statement, write a program which:
   a Reads the votes, one precinct at a time, for the three major candidates in the 1976 Presidential election
   b Totals the votes for all three candidates
   c At the operator's command will print out the total votes and the vote percentages for all three candidates

d Automatically returns to continuing to total the votes after each printout

3 Write a program to predict election results based on sample data.

CHEMISTRY

1 Write a program which converts Celsius to Fahrenheit degrees.

2 Write a program which will print grams/mole and atoms/mole from atomic weights and molecular formulas.

3 Write a program which computes the mass of a given radioactive element remaining after five intervals to half-lives in increments of 1/10 half-life.

PHYSICS

1 Write a program which will compute the distance light travels in x years.

2 A ball is thrown in the air with an initial velocity V at an angle A with the horizontal at a height D above the ground. Write a program which will plot the trajectory of the ball using n-second intervals until it hits the ground.

3 Write a program which converts common customary measurement units to metric units.

CALCULUS

1 Write a program which does integration by the trapezoidal rule.

2 Write a program to compute the zeros of a polynomial using Newton's method.

3 Write a program to approximate a limit.

ECONOMICS

1 Write a program to find marginal revenue, marginal cost, and total profit, given total revenue and total cost at each level of output.

2 Write a program which will compute the total interest earned, given the total invested, interest rate, number of years invested, and the number of times a year interest is paid.

3 Write a program to predict the average annual income for the next five years based on the past 20 years statistics on annual incomes.

BIOLOGY

1 Write a program to find the time between successive fissions if (a) there is no mortality; (b) 15 percent of cells originating from one fission die before the next, given that a logarithmically growing culture of bacteria increases from 2×10^6 cells to 3×10^8 cells in five hours.

2 The ABO blood groups in man are determined by a system of three alleles, A, B, and O. Genotypes AA and AO are group A; BB and BO are B; AB is group AB; and OO is group O. Write a program to determine whether the following proportions are consistent with the assumption of random mating. Given: 32.1 percent A, 22.4 percent B, 7.1 percent AB, and 38.4 percent O.

3 Write a program to print monthly biorhythms given month, day, and year of birth.

GAMES

1 Write a program which will play Tic Tac Toe.
2 Write a program which will simulate a slot machine.

3 Write a program which will simulate the game Battleship.

4 Write a program which will competitively play the old Chinese game of NIM.

BUSINESS

1 Write a program which will compare several depreciation methods.

2 Write a program to simulate car pool planning.

3 Write a program which provides stock market gains and losses for several stocks daily and weekly.

HUMANITIES

1 Write a program which will write poetry from a dictionary of words.

2 Write a program which will write a musical composition.

3 Write a program which will make a picture of some design.

CONSUMER LIVING

1 Write a program which computes miles per gallon and kilometers per liter.

2 Write a program which computes a bank account including deposits and expenditures. Include bank service charges.

3 Write a program which computes discounts and adds on sales tax to give final amount.

4 Write a program which computes and prints out costs, interest and down payments on an installment buying plan.

APPENDIX C
projects

WRITE A PROGRAM TO DO THE FOLLOWING:

1 Input a set of class test scores.
2 Find the mean.
3 Find the standard deviation.
4 Find the median.
5 Find the mode(s).
6 Print all class scores in groups as follows.

SCORES	FREQUENCY
90–100	
80–89	
70–79	
60–69	
50–59	
40–49	
30–39	
20–29	
10–19	
0– 9	

7 Assign a grade to each score as follows:

$$90-100=A$$
$$80-89=B$$
$$70-79=C$$
$$60-69=D$$
$$0-59=E$$

8 Rank the test scores from highest to lowest.
9 Print student's name or number, score and grade by ranked test scores; include labels for each.

NAME OR NUMBER	SCORE	GRADE
11427	98	A
11341	87	B
.	.	.
.	.	.
.	.	.

10 Print alphabetized class list including score and grade.
11 Print class title, test number, and date at top of alphabetized list.

COMPUTER SCIENCE I	TEST NUMBER 4	2/5/78
NAME	SCORE	GRADE
BITTER	98	A
GATELEY	87	B
.	.	.
.	.	.
.	.	.

PROJECT 2

TAKE HOME PAY

Write a program to do the following:

1 Input names of all company Y's employees.

2 Input total hours each worked for week R.

3 Input hourly wage for each employee.

4 Compute the wages "straight time" for the first 40 hours per week.

5 Compute wages time and a half for the hours over 40 hours per week.

6 Compute FICA at the present rate.

7 Compute federal and state withholding tax. Use 20% for federal and 8% for state.

8 Compute 15% for miscellaneous.

9 Create printout to include the following:

EMPLOYEE, HOURS, TOTAL GROSS WAGES, FEDERAL, STATE, FICA, MISC, NET PAY

10 Alphabetize the list and add date and company name to printout.

PROJECT 3

*INTERVIEW**

Here's an informative activity to do in a "Computers in Society" or "Computer Appreciation" course, or for that matter, in a social studies or sociology course.

EXERCISE 1

Make up copies of the interview form on the next page and give each student two copies. (You may want to use a subset of the questions instead of the entire list.) Each student should fill out one copy of the questionnaire himself/herself. Then, each student should interview an adult on these issues. Try to obtain interviews with a diverse cross-section of people. Students may feel more comfortable working in groups to get interviews; if so, let them pair off. But no more than two students to a group; more than that tends to overwhelm interviewees.

*Reprinted from CREATIVE COMPUTING, P.O. Box 789-˅M Morristown, New Jersey 07960 Nov–Dec 1974. Permission granted by *CREATIVE COMPUTING.*

EXERCISE 2

Tabulate the results, compare the various answers obtained, and discuss in class. Can you draw any conclusions about the attitude of the general public toward computers? Do students' attitudes generally agree or disagree with those of the interviewees? Are there any obvious relationships between the attitudes expressed and the demographic characteristics (age, sex, etc.) of the respondents?

EXERCISE 3

Write a computer program to tabulate the results and compute average scores for each question as well as percentage distributions.

CREATIVE COMPUTING
COMPUTERS AND SOCIETY QUESTIONNAIRE

Statement	Strongly Agree (1)	Mostly Agree (2)	Neutral or No Opinion (3)	Mostly Disagree (4)	Strongly Disagree (5)
1. Computers will improve health care.					
2. Computers will improve education.					
3. Computers will improve law enforcement.					
4. Computers slow down and complicate simple business operations.					
5. Computers are best suited for doing repetitive, monotonous tasks.					
6. Computers make mistakes at least 10 percent of the time.					
7. Programmers and operators make mistakes, but computers are, for the most part, error free.					
8. Computers dehumanize society by treating everyone as a number.					

CREATIVE COMPUTING
COMPUTERS AND SOCIETY QUESTIONNAIRE (Cont'd.)

Statement	Strongly Agree (1)	Mostly Agree (2)	Neutral or No Opinion (3)	Mostly Disagree (4)	Strongly Disagree (5)
9. It is possible to design computer systems which protect the privacy of data.					
10. Credit rating data stored on computers have prevented billions of dollars of fraud. This is a worthwhile use of computers.					
11. In the U.S. today, a person cannot escape the influence of computers.					
12. Computers will create as many jobs as they eliminate.					
13. Computers will replace low skill jobs and create jobs needing specialized training.					
14. Computers are a tool just like a hammer or lathe.					
15. Computers are beyond the understanding of the typical person.					
16. Computer polls and predictions influence the outcome of elections..					
17. Computers isolate people by preventing normal social interactions among people who use them.					

Age _____ Sex _____
Education _____
Occupation _____
Location _____
Name (optional) _____

EXERCISE 4

If your computer system has file capabilities, write a program to administer the questionnaire via a terminal, store the results and merge them with all previous results and then print out the scores to date. For real pizzazz, print the results graphically like this:

COMPUTERS WILL IMPROVE HEALTH CARE

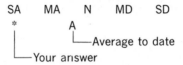

Or, show a bar chart of answers like this:

COMPUTERS DEHUMANIZE SOCIETY BY
TREATING EVERYONE AS A NUMBER

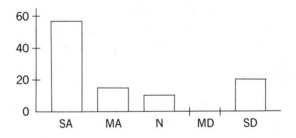

APPENDIX D
some system commands (can vary with different systems)

BYE   Computer will sign off and terminate communication

RUN   Instructs computer to compile and execute the program

NEW   Begins new program

OLD   Uses program storage previously assigned a file name

LIST   Prints out entire current program

LIST 20   Prints only line 20

LIST 20, 30 Prints out only lines 20 through 30 in current program

LISTNH   Prints out current program without heading

REPLACE Saves a program under the same name as the previously saved program

CATALOG Lists all active programs in file

LENGTH   Prints the number of characters in the program

SCRATCH Deletes program without changing the program name

SAVE   Saves the program under name assigned

UNSAVE   Unsaves the program
RENAME   Changes the name of the program to
                    name given after RENAME
                        i.e.   RENAME GARY program re-
                               named GARY
SEQUENCE   Automatically assigns line numbers
                        i.e.   SEQUENCE 20, 10 will start with
                               line number 20 and increase by 10
                               for each new line

APPENDIX E
some edit
commands
(could vary with
different systems)

1. EDIT DELETE

The EDIT DELETE command deletes selected lines from a program without having to type each line number separately.

Example A:

EDIT DELETE 10, 50
will delete lines 10 through 50 including 10 and 50

Example B:

EDIT DELETE 5, 25, 400
will delete lines 5 through 25 *and* lines 400 to the END including 5, 25, and 400

2. EDIT EXTRACT

The EDIT EXTRACT command will delete all lines from a program *except* those specified.

Example A:

> EDIT EXTRACT 10, 50
> > will eliminate all lines *except* 10 through 50

Example B:

> EDIT EXTRACT 5, 25, 200
> > will retain only lines 5 through 25 and 200
> > to the end

3. EDIT RESEQUENCE

The EDIT RESEQUENCE command will renumber
the lines in the program.

Example:

> EDIT RESEQUENCE 100, 43, 10, 78
> > will renumber program line 43 with 100
> > and will increase by 10 each time until line
> > 78 is reached

4. EDIT MERGE

The EDIT MERGE command is used to combine
several saved programs into one program.

Example: EDIT MERGE GARY, BITTER, 80
Program BITTER is inserted into Program GARY after line 80.

5. EDIT LIST

The EDIT LIST command lists specific steps of a
program.

Example A:

> EDIT LIST 45
> > lists line 45

Example B:

EDIT LIST 60, 90–100
  lists line 60 and all lines 90 to and including 100

6. EDIT PAGE

The EDIT PAGE command lists program in a paged format.

Example A:

EDIT PAGE GARY
  will list program GARY starting with page 1

Example B:

EDIT PAGE GARY, 10, BITTER, GLEN
  will list program GARY starting with page 10 and continue with Program BITTER followed by Program GLEN

INDEX

AF